Education to Better Their World

Unleashing the Power of 21st-Century Kids

Also by Marc Prensky

The World Needs a New Curriculum
Brain Gain: Technology and the Quest for Digital Wisdom
From Digital Natives to Digital Wisdom
Teaching Digital Natives: Partnering for Real Learning
Don't Bother Me Mom—I'm Learning
Digital Game-Based Learning

Education to Better Their World

Unleashing the Power of 21st-Century Kids

Marc Prensky

TEACHERS COLLEGE PRESS

TEACHERS COLLEGE | COLUMBIA UNIVERSITY

NEW YORK AND LONDON

Published by Teachers College Press, 1234 Amsterdam Avenue, New York, NY 10027

Library of Congress Cataloging-in-Publication Data

Names: Prensky, Marc, author.
Title: Education to better their world : unleashing the power of 21st-century kids / Marc Prensky.
Description: New York, NY : Teachers College Press, [2016] | Includes bibliographical references. | Description based on print version record and CIP data provided by publisher; resource not viewed.
Identifiers: LCCN 2016031467 (print) | LCCN 2016026988 (ebook) | ISBN 9780807774946 (ebook) | ISBN 9780807757901 (pbk.)
Subjects: LCSH: Education—Aims and objectives. | Educational change.
Classification: LCC LB41 (print) | LCC LB41 .P763 2016 (ebook) | DDC 370.11—dc23
LC record available at https://lccn.loc.gov/2016031467

ISBN 978-0-8077-5790-1 (paper)
ISBN 978-0-8077-7494-6 (ebook)

Printed on acid-free paper
Manufactured in the United States of America

23 22 21 20 19 18 17 16   8 7 6 5 4 3 2 1

For Sky and Rie
and for all children of the future

(and to JSB for I and R)

"What am I going to do
when it's time to help the world?"

—A high school student

Contents

Acknowledgments..ix

1. What's Happened...1

2. A Challenge to the World..8

3. Our New Globally Empowered Kids...12

4. Real, World-Improving Projects...15

5. Reuniting Our Two Great Educational Traditions:
   "Thinking" and "Accomplishing"..20

6. Education to Better Their World...24

7. What Kids Could Accomplish...35

8. Achievement vs. Accomplishment...50

9. *All* the Skills Kids Need...53

10. Supporting New Education with Technology............................71

11. The Changing Role of the Teacher
    in Educating Our Kids...84

12. Will Change Happen?..105

13. What People Can Do...112

Conclusion: Education as Rocket Science:
A New Metaphor   **119**

Appendix: Frequently Voiced (and Unvoiced) Concerns   **123**

Notes   **131**

About the Author   **134**

1. Teach with unknown
2. Self-evolving learners

3. Self-evolving organizes
    embrace constant change

Prepare kids for their future
not our past.

If we teach todo as
we taught yesterday
we rob our children

[handwritten: Innovative Explorer]

[handwritten: Industrial Age Model —]

[handwritten: Cognitosphere — Knowledge - Based Industry]

Acknowledgments

[handwritten: Where do we want to be — Why do we yield] *[handwritten: Dewey]*

Although the thoughts in this book are my own, I must thank a number of people who, through conversation and writing, contributed to this book in important ways.

I especially thank my closest collaborators, Esther Wojcicki and David Engle, for all their ideas and support.

Additional important ideas and contributions to my thinking came from Nick Morgan, Rob Berkley, John Seely Brown, Vint Cerf, Milton Chen, Pierre Cintra, Michael Fullan, James Paul Gee, David Hawley, Dan Keenan, Robert E. Levin, David Nordfors, Lionel de Rothschild, Tim Tien, James Tracy, my fine editor Jean Ward, and many others. Although I cannot remember, recognize, or acknowledge everyone's contribution, my apologies in advance to anyone who feels their name was (inadvertently) omitted from this list.

[handwritten: authentic reflection] *[handwritten: renovate Strengths + that - build]*

[handwritten: P. 123 Yes, but ....]

*[handwritten: → Grant Lichtman Tedx Denver
What 60 schools can tell us
About Teaching 21st Century Skills
Student -driven]*

[handwritten: Bloom's Taxonomy - how to learn]

THIS BOOK'S KEY MESSAGE

If you take away only one thing from this book, please let it be this thought:

> Our current education is wrong for the future *not* because we haven't added enough technology, or because we haven't added enough so-called 21st century skills, or because we don't offer it to everyone equally, or even because we haven't tried hard to incrementally improve it.
>
> Our current K–12 education is wrong for the future because it has—and we have—the wrong ends or goals, in mind. Up until now, education has been about improving individuals. What education should be about in the future is improving the world—and having individuals improve in that process.

IMPORTANT NOTE ON TERMINOLOGY

I use the term "K–12" education repeatedly in this book. It is a U.S.-centric term; much of the world uses the terms "primary education" and "secondary education" for the same thing. I use "K–12" only because it is shorter.

> **K–12 means *both* primary and secondary—*all* the years from kindergarten to the end of high school.**

Because the message in the book applies to the whole world, I ask that you make in your head the necessary language and cultural adjustments to your own particular context, whatever it may be.

Find people who share this view —

CHAPTER 1

What's Happened

JUST AT A TIME when "academic" education has spread around the globe, and we are struggling mightily to bring every kid into it, our world—and the things our kids are capable of doing in it—are changing radically.

Because the capabilities of our present and future kids are now so different, the education that we have universally been offering them throughout the world is no longer appropriate for the times in which they and their posterity will live. To succeed in the future, today's and tomorrow's young people require a different kind of start in the world—a different primary and secondary (K–12) education than the world now offers them.

Our kids now need an education that is far more connected and real than in the past—an education that gives them not only knowledge, but also provides them with empowerment and agency. They need an education whose ends are not just to improve themselves, but rather to improve the world they live in.

The outlines of this new and better education are now in the process of emerging in the world. At its core, it is **an education whose ends are to empower kids to improve their own world, starting when they are students.** Although this new education does not yet exist anywhere in its entirety—and will continue to emerge and evolve—its main elements are now showing up around the globe in more and more places in the ideas and practice of a growing number of individuals and groups. This book's purpose is to describe and highlight this new educational paradigm.

This emerging education benefits all of us—far more than the education of today. It benefits our kids more by enabling them to think more effectively (and far more practically) than our current education does, and, in addition, it empowers our kids to act, relate, and accomplish effectively in the world. It offers young people not just the pride and joy of real-world accomplishment, but all the self-confidence that comes with it. It arms kids who walk in an employer's door, or who apply to college, not just with a transcript of grades, but with a résumé of completed, real-world accomplishments.

↳ does this mean a need for a new kind of alternative school + curriculum.

If our educational system had been forced on us by a foreign country, we would have considered it an act of war.

It's also an education that benefits the world far more than the academic K–12 education of today. It benefits employers because they will get better prepared workers from the start. It benefits local and global society by unleashing a huge, as-yet-untapped potential world-improving force, as it elicits from our school-age kids real, implemented solutions to the existing problems and needs of our world.

Most important, it's an education that creates adults—future citizens—who already have experience, from their education, in finding and implementing real solutions to real problems. This is something that our current education not only does not do, but doesn't even *try* to do.

In this book, I offer my readers—who I hope will include a wide variety of people interested in education, from government leaders and politicians to educational policymakers, to parents, educational innovators, current and aspiring superintendents, school administrators and principals, graduate students of urban government and educational policy, teachers and teacher educators, members of the general public interested in and invested in providing children with the right education for our present and their future, and most importantly, many young people themselves— a new and alternate vision and perspective on how we can and should educate our offspring in their early (i.e., K–12) years. My goal is to convince you that a different kind of education is needed, that the vision and implementations of that vision are emerging, and that there is, in fact, a real and starkly different alternative—a far better one—to our current academic K–12 education. So much so that the two alternatives deserve very different names: the "Academic Model" of individual achievement in a narrow range of subjects (which is what we currently have) and the "Empowerment to Better the World Model" of liberating the newly acquired power of students to accomplish projects that improve their world (which is what is needed and where I believe we are going). Whether, as a world, we stick to academics for our students, or move to empower our kids to better their world, will have a profound impact on our future.

A BETTER APPROACH TO WORLD IMPROVEMENT

Improving the world has always been, of course, an *indirect* goal of education; but for some time it has become more of a by-product.

In the academic paradigm of education, we begin by putting students together with "content," hopefully producing some learning. Those students who learn become "better" people (almost entirely in an intellectual sense). The big bet of academic education—and our profound hope—is that those improved people will someday—typically long after their education—go out and improve the world.

But now we have available a much more direct means for our young people to reach the goal of improving their world— a goal they increasingly have and articulate. In this new, evolving educational paradigm we begin by putting students together not with content, but with problems. Not with problems educators make up, but with problems that the kids themselves perceive in their own world, both locally and globally. School then becomes about finding and implementing solutions to those real-world problems in ways that fully apply the strengths and passions of each kid—with the "content" being whatever, in a wide variety of realms, is needed along the way. The short-term positive result of this is *a better world immediately*. But the long-term result is far more powerful: We produce a population of adult citizens who have been empowered, by their education, to actually create solutions to real-world problems. Those adults will therefore go on creating real, world-improving solutions for the rest of their lives (Figure 1.1), becoming, in the language of educator Zoe Weil, "Solutionaries."[1]

Figure 1.1

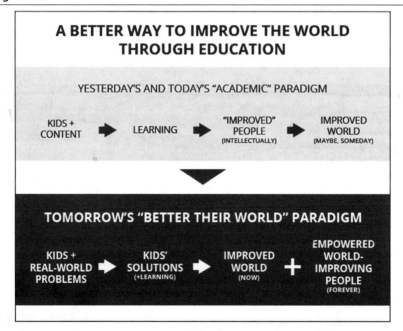

VISION VS. PRACTICE

This book is primarily about "vision" rather than "practice," and there is a very particular reason for that—what is needed at this point is a major shift in vision and mindset in the world about what K–12 education should be. It is crucial that all of us understand this need and think carefully about the bigger picture of change in the world, and how education must adapt.

Some people shift their mindset only after seeing numerous examples. This volume offers a number of real-world examples that are paradigmatic and indicative of things to come. It will be followed by a companion volume, describing in more detail the people and places moving toward that vision, and providing practical advice about various ways to get there.

In this book, I want to describe to readers—in all of the groups mentioned above—the vision of just what this better, emerging alternative education is. I hope to convince you *why* the new alternative is better, to briefly introduce to you some of the people who are already thinking and moving in these new directions, and to outline how, despite education's enormous resistance to change, we can get to this new education—to the immense future benefit of everyone in the world, both young and old.

Whether you are a leader, parent, educator, politician or student reading this, I hope to inspire you to join the movement toward a different and better K–12 education throughout the world.

WHY NOW?

The need for a new model of K–12 education stems, almost entirely, from the new and growing capabilities of our young people in the world, and our need to help our kids direct these new capabilities in positive ways. There are, no doubt, many ways to do this, but one way seems to be naturally emerging "bottom-up" in many places—the accomplishment of real, world-improving projects by school-age kids. The fact that so many of our kids are now capable of doing real, world-improving projects, in so many powerful new ways, is a new phenomenon in the world; one that our current education was not at all designed to encourage or help. So it is time for us to take a new and different approach.

A NEW PERSPECTIVE

A shift in vision and perspective is what lies at the root of any change, and that is what is really needed in K–12. And, of course, it must be followed up by new practices. But since all of us who are educated received the old-model academic education in some form, it is often hard for us to even *conceive* of something very different. We have not just been told, but been shown, from our youth, over many years, what a K–12 education is. When we hear of a different approach, many of us find it hard to see the new alternative as better, or to abandon much of the past. But it is crucial that we do so.

Our current K–12 education takes many forms in different places, but it has, at its core, only one unique proposition—to make individuals more effective at thinking (and not, for example, at action, relationships, or real-world accomplishment). No one disputes the importance of good thinking. But what has been lost over time is not just our success in making thinking happen effectively, but, more importantly, the narrowness of that mission in the scheme of all the things we want and need for our kids. It is also far from all that our kids themselves want—or need to be good at—to succeed in the world and to become the people they desire to be. Effective thinking—important as it is—is only a fraction of what kids need.

Reforms and attempts to improve our K–12 education also take myriad forms. But today too many of these are really only incremental changes to the old academic, "thinking-only"-based vision of education, which itself is no longer enough. Now, fortunately, we see a new path emerging—empowering our kids to better their world. And we see more and more people not only eager to take this new road, but already embarked upon it.

The coming implementations of the "Empowerment to Better Their World" vision will also take myriad forms. But they will all have, I believe, a few basic elements in common, and it is these common elements of the new educational vision that this book is about. Because the only way to tell whether something labeled as "reform" actually is—that is, whether it moves our education to a new and better place or is just an incremental upgrade to the past—is to have in your head the vision of where we should be going.

These are the common elements I believe the new Empowerment to Better Their World vision of K–12 education includes:

1. A shift in *Ends*: From educating individuals so that they can *someday* better their world, to actually bettering their world *as* their education.
2. A shift in *Means*: From academic learning and grades, to applying one's passion to real-world accomplishment.

3. A shift in *What We Expect All Kids to Become Good At* (i.e., our desired outcomes and essential curriculum for all): Away from math, language, science, and social studies as ends in themselves, to Effective Thinking, Action, Relationships, and Accomplishment in the real world.

4. A shift in *How We Teach*: From an academic approach of providing content and control, to an empowerment approach of coaching kids to accomplish effectively—through trust, respect, independence, collaboration, and kindness—along with powerful, and not just trivial, uses of technology.

I hope readers will leave this book with a better understanding and appreciation of how and why each of these elements is changing, how they fit together into a new vision of where K–12 education is now heading, and of the many benefits this new vision brings.

The structure of my argument, and the book, is as follows: This chapter sets out the underlying reason that we need fundamental change in our education—that our current system is wrong for the future, in ways that incremental improvements won't fix. Chapter 2 offers a challenge to those who might want to do things differently. Chapters 3 and 4 discuss our newly empowered kids and the kind of accomplishments they are now capable of (and eager to do). Chapter 5 highlights what has been left out of our education for the past several hundred years—i.e. real-world accomplishment—and how we can get it back by reconnecting our two great historical educational traditions. Chapters 6 through 8 describe what the new education looks like in its broad outlines, and helps distinguish between the "achievements" of the past and the "accomplishments" needed for the future. Chapter 9 lays out a structure for a better and far more comprehensive curriculum—not delivered lesson-by-lesson, as our current curricula mostly are, but a curriculum that underpins, is learned through, and supports real-world projects.

Once we begin to share the vision and understand why it is better, the next task is, of course, to get there. Chapter 10 describes a better and more helpful role for technology in doing this. Chapter 11 outlines an evolutionary path to the future for our teachers. Chapter 12 and the conclusion to this book discuss when change will happen and the benefits that we will all derive when it does.

At its core, this book is about a new, common vision for education, particularly K–12 education. It is about how the fragmented elements of a future vision are now coming together, allowing people who want fundamental change to finally say, "I don't choose the educational vision of the past (and today); I choose the educational vision of tomorrow." (Or, "I don't choose just an old (or updated) academic education for my kid (or for myself). I choose an education that Betters the World.")

St. Augustine is reputed to have said, "In essentials unity, in all else liberty, and in all things charity." The essentials, in this case, are the basic elements of the new common vision of K–12 education around which the world is starting to unify. The liberty is in the great multitude of implementations of this new common vision, implementations that are now emerging in a variety of different forms all over the globe. The charity—hugely important—is the fresh and more respectful way that we are, slowly, beginning to view our newly empowered kids.

CHAPTER 2

A Challenge to the World

IMAGINE reading or hearing about the following decree from some country's Department or Ministry of Education at the end of a school year:

———

In the coming year, education in [our country] will be completely new and different. It will not be about subjects and grades at all. Education will be about—and only about—improving our country and our communities.

During the entire year, every student and every teacher in our country will focus all their efforts on a series of real-world projects—projects that make our country a better place in some way.

We will not define or create these projects—the students and teachers will. Some may do so as classes, others as teams of students and teachers within and across classes—and, when possible, even countrywide. To get approved and started, projects will need to meet only one criterion: "Show us how this will improve some aspect of our country."

Each project will create its own very specific goals, which can range from improving a neighborhood's appearance or function, to improving a community's infrastructure, preserving part of our country's history and heritage, helping out local government and regulators, making life better for our less fortunate, building new relationships between people in real (and online) communities, adding or improving technology, and to what we hope will be many more good ideas. The only limit is the creativity and resourcefulness of the teams. Projects can last for weeks (e.g., "Let's turn that ugly piece of land into a community garden"), or months (e.g., "Let's create the best Wi-Fi in the country in our school and/or neighborhood"), or the entire year (e.g., "Let's stop or slow the increase of some disease in our community"). Students may do several projects over the course of the year. Projects will be based entirely on applying the passions of team members to helping the country in whichever way they think best, and they will need to produce positive results and progress toward their ultimate goals within the year. Teams can be teacher driven, student driven, or both. Teams can enlist the private sector, government agencies, or nongovernmental organizations (NGOs) as partners in creative ways.

Every student and teacher in our country will participate. There will be little structure and regulation—we count on the creativity of our students and teachers to set this up and make it work. Only minimal guidelines will be promulgated. Everyone now has the summer to think about this. By the end of the first month of school, we expect every teacher and student to have created or signed up for their first team, and to have begun their projects.

We will create a website for keeping track of all the projects, and make sure every school can access it by either computer or phone. Completed projects will be evaluated by online voting as being either: (1) something that made the country better (which we expect will be almost all of them), (2) something that made the country outstandingly or exceptionally better (perhaps 10% of the projects), and (3) projects that did not succeed in improving the country, with recommendations on how to change them so that they do (we hope this number will be quite small).

This initiative's motto—and our country's educational mission for the next school year—will be this and only this:

> You can make our country better—
> surprise us with how much you—and we—can do.

———

Now imagine this had actually happened somewhere, and it is a year later. What might be the result?

- Would that country have improved?
- Would those in charge now have a great many ideas on how to make the country improve even more the following year?
- Would the country's students, having completed these nation- and community-improving projects, be better off in terms of their self-confidence, effectiveness, enthusiasm, and participation in their education?
- Would the country's teachers be better off in terms of their enthusiasm and participation?

- Would students have learned lots of useful and relevant information by seeking it out on their own to help their projects?
- Or, would it all have become a big mess, with the kids just losing out from missing a year of academic instruction?

I don't know the answer. But if I had the appropriate power, I would do the experiment. What we are doing today as K–12 education does very little to benefit and improve our kids, or our communities, countries, and world, compared to what it could do. We need to do better.

COULD IT HAPPEN?

There are some who doubt that a challenge like this, even if accepted, would produce much change at all. Their main argument is that people like and expect to be "told what to do" and not to act on their own toward goals they set themselves. In a great many places, these people argue, neither our students nor our teachers are ready for the concept of "agency"—that is, of taking responsibility for improving their own world. For people like this, it is a huge and difficult change in perspective.

But I think a lot more kids are ready than most think.

"DON'T EXPERIMENT WITH *MY* KID"

If a minister (or someone else in authority) did initiate the challenge described above, he or she would no doubt have to face hordes of angry parents shouting things like, "Don't experiment with *my* kid!" or "I want my kid to have the exact same education I did (only better!)." Many parents are already shouting this today.

Were I that minister (or superintendent, or whatever) my answer to those parents, would be this:

I understand your concerns, but we *have to* experiment and find a better way. Your kids live in a new world that is very different from the one our generation grew up in. Today's young people are far more empowered than kids were in the past—they have enormous new capabilities that kids have never had before. We truly don't yet know how to best educate these empowered kids in their new environment.

But we do know that our current education—even with marginal improvements—is no longer working as it used to. So *not* to experiment to find better ways to educate these kids would be irresponsible. I'm sure you are all responsible parents—and I'm a responsible educator—so let's get on with our experiments, because we are all in a new age.

OUR NEW AGE OF EXPLORATION

For roughly 200,000 years, up until more or less the end of the first millennium (that is, somewhere around 1000 A.D., very approximately) humans were agricultural animals. Almost everyone in the world was a farmer or herder of some kind. Humans had a very long agricultural age during which all kids pretty much knew—with only the most minor exceptions—that they would be doing the same agricultural and fieldwork as their father or parents. In what we now call the first millennium A.D. most of the world's people were still in that stage.

The following millennium—the second millennium that has just ended—was different. It was an age, particularly in its last centuries, of huge construction and development. During this millennium, our great cities were expanded, industrialization was born, great inventions were created, and great infrastructures were built. The kids who grew up in the second millennium grew up in an age of building. It was, as well, an age of discoveries, but only for relatively few individual explorers and intrepid pioneers.

We are entering, in this so-called third millennium, a new age of exploration—one far different than what we saw in the past. One of the biggest differences is that now almost everyone can participate in the explorations and discoveries of their times. Kids who grow up in the third millennium will explore and not just the Earth, but outer space. They will explore and understand the human mind and brain as never before, and they will explore the new kind of worlds—digital and virtual—that are still being born. They will help solve the problems that our planet and our species face, as people never could in the past.

What is most exciting is that kids can now start these processes of exploring, solving the world's problems, and making their world a better place in their early and formative years, instead of waiting to become adults before doing so. That is a big change for all of us.

CHAPTER 3

Our New Globally Empowered Kids

IT IS NO EXAGGERATION to say that the world's kids today, aged roughly 6–18, are the most disrespected, underappreciated, and underestimated, and yet—potentially—the most powerful group in the world for our future.

Why do I say that?

The "disrespected" part is easy. In most countries, including certainly my own, the United States, we treat our kids with virtually no respect at all. We hardly listen to them, or even try to. We give them goals that are almost exclusively our goals, not theirs. We tell them where to go and what to do, pretty much exactly. We reward them not for being independent or individuals, but for conforming to our "standards." I know this because, in over 40 countries, kids have told me so. On the student panels I conduct around the world, the number one request from students is for more respect from adults.

The "underappreciated" part is also not very hard to see. Whenever there are choices to be made between kids doing things that they want to do and know they can, and things we want kids to do, the choice is clear. We rarely give kids credit for all the organizational and other tasks they can accomplish with their new technologies, or even the opportunity to use them. We expect their whole educational life to be in the classroom and in school-related activities—any educational initiative kids take outside of the confines of their classroom and curriculum is generally not expected and rarely rewarded. Very occasionally, kids may be asked to do a real-world "service project" (more often in private than public schools) over which they may have some minor degree of control, but mostly we care about—and reward—only their academic achievements. We rarely reward, or even evaluate real-word accomplishment, because it is so rare in our system.

I call today's kids "underestimated" because we hardly ever let them realize the full potential of what they can do—particularly to improve the world. Rarely do we ask our kids to find real problems—much less fix or solve them—mostly because we think this is a job for adults. Only the very best teachers have the courage to say to their kids, "Surprise me," and give them open parameters to do so.

Although there are certainly exceptions, what I say applies to the vast majority of kids in the world—almost all of them, in fact. Even in our "best" schools, kids often grow up disrespected, underappreciated, and undervalued by their educators, except in the narrowest of ways. Again, I know this because they tell me so.

ANOTHER WAY

It doesn't have to be like that. In this new technological age, we are starting to see around the world the beginnings of a new kind of empowered young person, with a new relationship with their educators and with their educations. For the moment, it may only be glimmers here and there, but the cumulative effect is very powerful. It will, I predict, become stronger and eventually the norm—*if* the kids learn to believe in and use their new power, and *if* we don't continue to do our best to—and succeed at—squashing it (although I think it's too late for that).

The "Globally Empowered Kids" I am talking about are those who have realized that when they see a problem in the world, they don't have to wait—or get permission—to begin solving it. They can take matters into their own hands and begin fixing the problem. ("It's just me, doing what I think is right" says one.[2]) They are the young people who, with technology and without it, now repair perceived wrongs, fix broken infrastructure, redistribute used products, teach each other skills, build networks, design parks, repair the environment, write official reports. They are both "Globally Empowered Kids," who can act around the world, and "Global Empowered Kids" in that they can be found almost everywhere. They refuse to spend their youth just playing the old school game. Sometimes they drop out, but often they just change their priorities. Many of them are now balancing between doing the old and being empowered, just waiting for the scales to tip.

EXTENDED MINDS ALL NETWORKED TOGETHER

We need to see these kids as they increasingly see themselves: as "extended minds all networked together."

Their extended minds reside to a great extent in the devices that more and more of them carry with them (principally and increasingly smartphones, connected to and through other powerful devices such as clouds, computers, and gaming consoles). These new devices allow kids not only to *take in* information (as they could with reading) and create reports (as they could with writing), but to combine, analyze, and manipulate information in very new ways. On their devices, students can now:

- collaborate with people anywhere, often in real time;
- combine and analyze world databases (e.g., through wolframAlpha, one of whose interfaces is Siri on the iPhone);
- simulate trillions of trials of systems and populations;
- extend their reach through robotics and artificial intelligence;
- discover previously unknown information about the far reaches of the galaxy or the microstructure of the brain;
- poll large groups of people, around the world, about any topic.

And they can do so much more that is new (see my book *Brain Gain*). Today, almost every kid in the world knows about these devices and wants one (or a better one). We are fast approaching the time when all will have them.

By "all networked together," I mean the totality of the technology-based social connection that these devices enable.

We need a new model of education that liberates the power of these "extended minds all networked together," without trapping them in the vicious cycles of academic competition that we often see in today's schools. Today, we see far too many kids disengaging themselves from the education we provide. Even more discouraging is that we have seen—not just in one place but in places around the world—that when we push kids too far in the directions much of our current academic education is going (i.e., extreme pressure to achieve within our current curriculum, and to do well at high-stakes testing) some of them, literally, prefer to die. In places from Singapore to South Korea to Silicon Valley kids are, literally, committing suicide because of academic pressure.[3]

Is that what our young people deserve? Is that the kind of education that we want and they need? We can do so much better.

CHAPTER 4

Real, World-Improving Projects
10 Favorite Examples

ONE OF THE MOST POWERFUL WAYS in which we can do better for our Globally Empowered Kids is to help them apply their newly acquired powers to projects that better their world. It is important to understand what these world-improving projects are and how they differ from the kinds of projects kids do in school today.

Real, world-improving projects are *projects that produce actual, and hopefully lasting, changes in our kids' local and global communities—changes that they can point to and say, "I—with my team—did that!"*

Today, most of the projects that kids do in class—even those that are called "real"—do not affect the world outside of the classroom at all. Almost all of them are made up, mostly by teachers, to achieve learning goals and meet learning standards. Such projects may, in fact, help the kids learn in more engaging ways. But they make no difference whatsoever in their world. Calling the projects "authentic" doesn't help at all, because authentic means only "real-like." Examples of such authentic-but-fake projects include research that leads to never-implemented recommendations, or reports to some group that are never taken seriously, or form-letter-answered letters to politicians, or even publications that only a few ever see. That is not what I mean by a real, world-improving project—*even if* the recommendations or report get submitted to some official group. It becomes "real-world" *only* if it is done for a real audience *and* leads to action and a difference in the world.

There are already a great many such real, world-improving student projects that have been accomplished around the world, and I am working to create a global database of such projects (at www.globalempoweredkids.org)

15

for all to use. If you know of any project(s) that should be included, I hope you will email me at marcprensky@gmail.com.

SOME FAVORITE EXAMPLES

Meanwhile, here are 10 of my favorite real, world-improving projects as I write this. You can see the growing number of these projects at www.globalempoweredkids.org.

1. When three teenage siblings in Decatur, Georgia, aged 14, 15, and 16, thought that their family had been unfairly harassed by the police, they said to themselves, "Why don't we create an app to help us solve this problem?" Using coding skills they had developed online, they created a mobile phone app for citizens to use to rate their encounters with the police (and other public servants), allowing people to compare communities. Their Five-O mobile app empowers citizens, according to the Google Play site from which it can be downloaded, (https://play.google.com/store/apps/details?id=com.five_o), "to record and store data from every encounter with law enforcement." Those incident reports are then electronically collated and analyzed' and can be shared and used by communities to rate individual officers and police departments as a whole. Not only has the app received wide publicity, but also numerous suggestions for improving the app have been posted on the Google Play site. A video about the app is at www.huffingtonpost.com/2014/08/18/teens-police-brutality-app_n_5687934.html.[4]
2. Three middle school girls in Columbia, South Carolina, printed prosthetic hands on a 3D printer using files freely available on the website of a nonprofit organization e-NABLE (www.enablingthefuture.org/). The girls then used the Internet to find other kids who needed such prosthetics and custom-designed a hand for each of them, distributing the hands at a "hand-a thon" event (a video is at www.3dprint.com/70224/girl-power/). Similar events have now spread to many schools.[5]
3. A 14-year-old boy in Washington DC noticed that restaurants visited by his family threw away all the crayons that had been given to kids waiting for their meals. Inspired by what he had

learned in an after-school entrepreneurship class, yoni Kalin started a nonprofit organization called Color My World to collect, sanitize, and redistribute the used crayons to kids who couldn't afford them, organizing volunteer middle school, high school, and college students to commit their time to this cause. (Find more at www.colormyworldproject.org). A video is at www.colormyworldproject.org/press/.[6] Additional examples of student entrepreneurs are listed in Chapter 7.

4. A fourth-grade class of 9-year-olds in North Platte, Nebraska, was informed by their teacher of the local community's "Request for Proposal" for a new water park. They responded by forming teams to design the water park to their own needs. They lobbied the city council and ultimately got their ideas incorporated into the plans of the architectural firm that was awarded the contract.[7]

5. A high school class in Westlaco, Texas, heard from an instructor that the Arecibo radio telescope—one of the largest satellite dishes in the world—was becoming inaccurate because of algae and debris accumulation. Under the guidance of the instructor, who put them in touch with the Arecibo scientists, they began designing a complex robotic system, currently in the prototype stage, to clean and maintain the enormous dish.[8]

6. High school students in Port Townsend, Washington, saw many of the old wooden sailing boats in their historic sailing and maritime community falling into disrepair because of lack of maintenance. Wanting to make their education more real by linking up their schools to their community, they began a project to connect to their historic traditions by restoring those boats under the guidance of the community's old master craftsmen.[9]

7. A sixth-grade class of 12-year-olds, hearing that their school was mandated to submit an environmental report, volunteered to do the report in place of the previous year's high-priced consultants. The school accepted their bid and the report was submitted to and accepted by the government authorities, becoming far more than "just an exercise."[10]

8. Two high school students in Colorado designed and built a custom robotic controller that allowed a severely disabled 7-year-old student to attend classes remotely. The student used their specially designed pressure-sensitive pillow—which

was all he could physically manage with his disability—to
control a commercial computer on wheels in and out of his
classes. (A video is at www.dcsdk12.org/community-relations/
job-alike-robotic-students.)[11]

9. A 6-year-old in Ontario, Canada heard from his teacher
   that many schools in Africa lacked clean water and proper
   sanitation. While still in grade one, he founded the Ryan's
   Well Foundation, whose volunteers have now dug more
   than 1,000 wells bringing access to clean water and better
   sanitation to more than 714,000 people in 16 countries.
   (A video is at www.youtu.be/jvPftkOfmFY. More can be found
   at www.ryanswell.ca.)[12]

10. After budget cuts eliminated the positions of government-
    funded water monitors, high school kids at High Tech
    High in San Diego, California, learned to use the complex
    water-monitoring equipment that the government had
    purchased but which was sitting idle after the testing budget
    was canceled. The students resumed the highly useful water
    monitoring, and when the government wouldn't "officially"
    accept data from the students, they published the data online
    for the community to use.[13]

What is characteristic of each of these projects is that they do more
than just help kids learn. Learning is, of course, involved, but learning
is not the "ends" of the projects. The ends, and what is important, is
that kids are accomplishing something useful that is *making their world
better,* and are learning in the process of doing so.

LEARNING, BY ITSELF, IS NOT EDUCATION

Today, "learning" is at the top of the agenda of those who see themselves as educators. I frequently hear the phrase, "Learning to learn is
the most important skill kids can have" in public statements. Without
diminishing the usefulness of learning, and of helping kids to learn,
I think we err in putting learning at the top of the pyramid of what
kids need and what education is about. I believe "accomplishing" is
the primary skill that all people need, and that learning is merely one
means toward accomplishment. Even learning to accomplish something
is not enough—you actually have to do it.

As humans, we cannot help learning—everybody learns as they go through life. But, not everybody accomplishes. In fact, far fewer do than we would like.

I believe the best way to view education is as the process of preparing our kids to reach their—and not necessarily our—goals. The skill they most need to do this is accomplishing, in whatever area(s) they are passionate about—with learning as an enabling means to do so. As adults, I believe we have a responsibility to our kids to help them direct their learning toward the accomplishments that will be the most helpful to reaching their goals in the future. I very much hope their goals will include becoming, in some highly individual way, a good, effective, and world-improving person. I further believe—and I think the young people in the world believe, perhaps today more than in the past—that education should direct their abilities to better not just their own lives, but also their world. Not as we see the world, but as they see it.

So *learning,* as an end in itself, is not—and should not be, I believe— our students' primary goal, or the primary goal of their education. I suggest we focus less on learning as the goal of our educational discussions and practice, and more on giving our kids the best preparation we can for them to achieve their goals. That means making sure their education consists of real-world accomplishments. The goals of those accomplishments should be to better their world.

The primary goal of education should be real, world-improving accomplishment, with learning as an enabling skill.

That, I believe, is the new model of education that is emerging.

CHAPTER 5

Reuniting Our Two Great Educational Traditions: "Thinking" and "Accomplishing"

MANY THINK that the academic process and learning model is the only educational tradition we have—and the only way education can be delivered. But there are actually *two* great historical educational traditions in the world.

The first, oldest, and broadest is the one-to-one, parent-to-child, master-to-apprentice, mentor-to-mentee tradition. It goes back, I suspect, as far as the human race. People showed other people, mostly one at a time, how to think, act, relate, and accomplish in effective ways. People used this kind of education to get things done, and those people taught others how to get things done—most often by showing and doing. They raised large workforces and armies, built enterprises and learned to manage them—passing that knowledge along one-to-one. They formed guilds and other organizations to preserve and disseminate (to those they judged worthy) what they knew. When writing was invented, they used it for accounting, planning, building, and keeping records.

The second great tradition began when certain individuals began to care about the world in particular thoughtful and thought-related ways. Some of these people wanted to understand the world better. Some wanted to explore our relationship to god(s) and spirituality more deeply. Some wanted to understand people and thinking better. Some wanted to create new knowledge. While thinking, of course, is universal—everyone does it— disciplined thinking, i.e., thinking that follows certain useful and rigorous patterns, rules, and procedures, has to be learned and practiced. That particular area became the province and specialty of this tradition and group. Over time, they established forums, universities, and religious orders, often deliberately exclusive.

They gathered disciples, who helped share and disseminate their thoughts. They passed on to each other what they knew and had learned, often in group settings and often with great ritual. When writing was invented, they captured what they knew and collected it in libraries, great and small, religious and secular.

We can call these two traditions, if you will, the "accomplishment" and the "academic" (or "thinking") traditions of education. The two have developed separately over the centuries. Today the two traditions have wound up in separate spaces. The academic tradition has gone to our schools, and therefore to our kids, and the accomplishment tradition has gone into our workplaces, and therefore to our adults.

The result is that, in many cases, our people now need *two* educations. After kids have completed their academic education in schools, the workplace often serves as a second, needed education that shows them how to accomplish and add value to the world—something that our schools do not currently do. More and more employers are complaining about the fact that they have to re-educate people in order to get them to add value after all those years they have spent in school. It's a combination of skills taught in school not being applied, and skills needed for accomplishment not being taught. This is an incredibly inefficient—and increasingly ineffective—way to educate our kids. It's both wasteful and unnecessary.

We need, for our future world, to bring the two traditions back together. We need to re-forge the broken link between our academic achievement-oriented education and our real-world, accomplishment-oriented education—between our schools and our adult jobs and professions. Today we are already seeing start-ups emerging in the world that attempt to combine the traditions, by giving unemployed or underemployed kids and adults skills that are useful in the workplace, and by helping people recognize useful skills they already possess, identify what skills they may be missing, and find ways to acquire them. For example:

- *Freeformers,* a company in the United Kingdom, shows adults from all walks of life how skills they already possess can be useful to businesses.
- *Potential.ly,* also a company in the United Kingdom, helps people better understand their personality in order to maximize their potential.

Now, finally, the world is beginning to find a way to bring the two traditions together in our schools—by having our kids' education be about real-world accomplishment.

A crucial barrier we need to overcome in re-combining these two great traditions into one education is the mistrust that each side, over time, has developed toward the other. As school expanded to larger populations, many academics came to believe that "real education" was only about developing the mind, viewing whatever was *not* about thinking as having lesser value. And many "accomplishers" saw school as not doing enough to help kids prepare for the real world, and as not giving kids all the skills they needed to accomplish their goals. Some academics began calling anything in education that *wasn't* primarily about thinking by other names, such as "training." Hugely important skill sets in the world, such as acting, relating, and accomplishing were ignored, or given lesser importance, in our school settings, often labeled "general," "second track," or "vocational." (The irony here is that academic education is, in a sense, "vocational training for intellectuals.") Today, kids who do well at academics are often encouraged to take *nothing but* academic and advanced placement classes. Action and relationship skills are often referred to, derogatorily, as "soft." With rare exceptions, the academics never allow or bring in, in a serious way, experts in the kind of accomplishment that takes place in the real adult world—except for a few lesser-valued "shop" and "trade" courses, like auto mechanics or machine shop. While some places—particularly in Europe—created two-track systems, the vocational track is often viewed by academics as "lesser." Respected, real-world accomplishment has became almost nonexistent in our academic schools.

As a result, what emerged in too many of our schools is the false notion *that thinking is all that education is about.* So more and more businesses, recognizing that most accomplishment skills were lacking in K–12 education, started formal education programs of their own.

BRINGING THE TWO TRADITIONS BACK TOGETHER

The way things have evolved is not helpful. It is not even close to the best we can do at a time when our kids can suddenly accomplish so much. There needs to be a better way to combine the thinking and the accomplishing traditions, and that is where I believe we are heading. Now, at the start of the third millennium, the K–12 model of education is changing, slowly but inexorably, from being just about the thinking tradition of education, to combining the thinking and accomplishing traditions in a new way—through real-world projects.

The model of K–12 education is changing from kids just learning about the world to actually improving it while they are students.

This is good for all of us.

CHAPTER 6

Education to Better Their World
The New Ends and Means of the Emerging Alternative for K–12 Education

IN SUM, what we offer our kids as K–12 education in the world today is the wrong education for their future. Fortunately, the right kind of education is emerging and the map is becoming clear.

What more and more people are beginning to see is that our current education is wrong *not* because we haven't added enough technology, or because we haven't added enough so-called 21st-century skills, or because we don't offer it to everyone equally, or even because we haven't tried hard to incrementally improve it.

Our current K–12 education is wrong for the future because it has—and we have—the wrong ends or goals in mind. We—the entire world—have an outdated idea about the purpose of an education in the third millennium. Up until now, education has been about improving individuals. What education should be about in the future is improving the world, and having individuals improve in that process.

WHY NEW ENDS?

For centuries, formal education—whether delivered through apprenticeship or through the now universal academic model of schools, classrooms, teaching, courses, and grades—has been about individual improvement and achievement. The assumption is that if each individual, on his or her own, learns the basics and makes the most progress he or she can, then when their education is finished they will be ready to go out and lead better individual lives, and hopefully (but by no means certainly) improve the world.

The ends or goals of improving individuals may once have been the right ones for the world and for our kids. But they are no longer the right ends for the future.

In the future, the purpose of education—the reason we educate our young—can be and has to be to improve their world. Not indirectly—some day when the kids are adults—but immediately, while our kids are being educated, as an immediate and direct result of that process.

Why is it time for this big switch in the ends of education? First, because the world needs it—we can no longer afford to waste a large percentage of our human potential to improve the world we live in while we wait for our kids to grow up. And second, because with technology it is now possible to do world improvement by kids at scale. Today, if we are willing to make it happen, school kids can improve the world—at almost no incremental cost, and with enormous incremental benefit—in ways that weren't possible before. The connection between academic learning success and actually improving the world is tenuous at best. The connection between real-world accomplishment as students, and improving the world as adults, is much more direct.

KIDS ADDING VALUE

Yet today, at a time when the world needs all the help it can get, we literally ignore and effectively throw away the new potential value-adding power of those in school—a significant proportion of all humans. The waste is perhaps greatest in the kids' younger years, because we have somehow decided that these young human beings have no value to add to the world through our educational system until we have taught them, and they have grown up.

However, as seen in the examples in Chapter 4 and elsewhere, the young today are no longer buying this specious argument, and neither should we.

Today's kids, around the world, know they can add value to the world right now. And they are, in more and more cases, going out and doing it, either on their own or—when they are lucky—supported by adults and programs.

Primary school kids are inventing new products to make people safer, such as by figuring out new ways to desalinate water.[14] Ten- and 11-year-olds are inventing ways to help overcome natural disasters[15] and doing government work such as cryptography.[16] High school kids are inventing ways to make plastic from waste, installing and upgrading networks, testing water quality, and restoring historic artifacts. Kids of all ages and genders are starting companies and not-for-profit organizations to solve world problems, and sharing what they do and know with other kids via YouTube. What is currently being done by kids is already amazing, but their potential has hardly been tapped.

We are at the start of something completely new and positive—school-age kids able to improve the world in useful, measurable, and nonexploitive ways. What we now need—above all—from our education is to encourage this further.

WHY NOW?

We have entered a time when huge technological and societal changes are happening at an enormously accelerating rate—a time when much of what used to take decades now happens, literally, in nanoseconds—and a world in which attitudes, fixed for generations, are changing (e.g., about privacy) almost overnight. Although there are many unknowns on which we should be keeping a watchful eye, this new environment and context has already begun to empower our kids in ways never before seen in the world. Both *technology* and *context* are quickly extending our young people's minds and capabilities, giving them powers that are completely new. Consider all the capabilities—from video, to calculation, to search, to translation, to super-computing, to geolocation—already in many kids' pockets, and now imagine the power that will be there tomorrow. And the greatest empowerment of all comes from the rapidly growing *connectivity* of our young people—connecting with each other, with all the world's knowledge, and with everyone on the planet. We now have the world's first truly horizontal, globally connected generation. We must learn to educate these young people for their future world.

The idea of "brain plasticity"—that brains change in response to their surroundings and inputs—is one of the last quarter-century's great new understandings from neuroscience. We are still learning about how our kids' "plastic" brains are reacting to their new environment. But we know for sure that the young people whom it is now our task to educate can usefully be thought of as "extended minds, all networked together," with whom we have to explore jointly. They are no longer the young people we were—that is, kids who need to be taught by adults before they can act. They are people who have the power—while they are still kids, and with proper guidance—to vastly improve the world personally, locally, and globally.

A NEW MINDSET

That is precisely what their education should be about: empowering them further, and helping them to apply their individual and collective passion to making their world a better place. Our education should have as its ends world improvement and making each young person into a good, effective, and world-improving adult.

We already have the tools we need to do this, but we lack the mindset. Education throughout in the world is stuck in an academic mindset of "learn first, act in the world later." This academic mentality has completely taken over education in the past several hundred years.

Today, academic education is ubiquitous in the world—albeit with a wide range of quality and success. It is, in fact, the *only* formal education we have. Our current education asks of our newly empowered kids pretty much the same things we have been asking kids for the last hundred years: to learn content and skills in a narrow, prescribed range of subjects, to achieve academically, to get good grades, to succeed in the system (i.e., to graduate) and even—in this new age of networks—to "do their own work" and achieve individually.

"THE MESS"

Our academic K–12 education is based, almost universally, on a narrow core curriculum of math, language, science, and social studies. The acronym for these subjects in the English-speaking world is "**MESS**" (for **M**ath, **E**nglish, **S**cience, and **S**ocial studies)—and it is certainly apt. Academic education is based, fundamentally, on the premise of "learn the MESS first, so that you can accomplish later." Pretty much everything that goes on today under the name of education reform is about doing academic education and the MESS better: by serving more underserved kids, by adding new types of schools (e.g., charter schools), by adding more STEM (science, technology, engineering, and math) courses, by adding so-called 21st century skills, or by adding more and more technology.

THE ACADEMIC EDUCATION OF YESTERDAY IS NO LONGER SUFFICIENT—EVEN IF WE INCREMENTALLY IMPROVE IT

But an improved academic education is not what today's and tomorrow's empowered kids want or need—it no longer fits the world in which these kids live. These increasingly empowered kids need an education that empowers them further. They need, want (and deserve) an education that enables them to make their world a better place. They need an education that moves from the academic model of "learn now so you can accomplish later" to a new model of "accomplish now and learn as you do." They need an education that allows them, while they are still students, to be continually accomplishing projects that improve the world, locally and globally. They need an education that enables them to make their world better—i.e., a "Better Their World" education, if you will. And, fortunately, Education to Better Their World is now beginning to emerge in the world.

EDUCATION TO BETTER THEIR WORLD: BETTER FOR KIDS, BETTER FOR US

What we can now be asking—and should be asking of our future, empowered kids—is that they become educated through actually improving their world, in whatever way inspires them, by fully utilizing and applying their unique passions and skills—and not, any longer, through learning mostly predetermined bodies of knowledge and skills that might possibly be used later. We should be asking them—and teaching them—to improve their world now, while they are still in school—not someday, when they become adults. We should be asking them to complete an education based on their personal applied passions, and not on a universal, narrow, MESS-based curriculum.

Improving their personal, local, and global worlds is precisely what today's young people *want* to do and what they *can* do with their newly enhanced power and connectivity. It is certainly what the world needs. Imagine (as we did at the start of this book) that any country declared that its education in the future would be *only* about improving that country—utilizing student power to do so in myriad ways (and having students improve through that process). How much could that country improve?

Today, we don't formally have our kids better their world *as* their education anywhere in the world. But we could—and should—do this in the future. That is what kids want, it is what the world needs, and that is what our K–12 education should be. Our kids need and deserve a Better Their World education.

AN "APPRENTICESHIP TO THE WORLD"

Better Their World education is in a sense a third-millennium combination of the 2 models that served as education for thousands of years, before the academic model took over our schools. It is about students, in a 21st century sense, "apprenticing to the world"—using all their new powers and connectivity to become people who can accomplish effectively—before leaving school.

What enables our young people to improve their world is not just their passion, but their *applied passion*. This new, real-world accomplishment-based education lets kids apply their passion, whatever it may be, both to solving world problems and to becoming the people they want to be and what we want them to be—good, effective, and world-improving in their own areas of interest. The new education is designed to help kids to identify their areas of interest early, to truly understand their unique passions and capabilities, and to connect those interests, capabilities, and passions to the kind of real-world projects that stretch them to reach their full potential as human beings.

The Empowerment to Better Their World Model—is a far better education both for tomorrow's kids and for us. It is better for kids because it offers them—in addition to knowledge and skills—independence, applied passion, and a strong sense of accomplishment, along with a strong sense of how they fit into the future world. It is far better for us because it liberates huge amounts of unused potential—the potential of our students—to improve our communities and our planet.

NEVER BEFORE FEASIBLE

A real-world, project-based K–12 education that empowers kids to Better Their World was not feasible in the past—our kids were too powerless and isolated. But in the new era of empowered kids, and extended minds all networked together, empowering our kids to accomplish in the real world is the best, and perhaps the only way to take our education forward. The old academic, individual, "learn before you do" model of education—is dying. The world is giving birth to a new model for K–12 education.

Better Their World education is not, as yet, fully implemented anywhere, but it is definitely coming. We are beginning to see the elements of this new education emerging, at all levels, in scattered places and pockets around the globe. We are seeing districts and programs whose goal is improving the world. We are seeing real-world projects happening *as* the education, in professional schools like medicine and business, in the workplace, in colleges, and recently in K–12 schools, both private and public. We are seeing new curricula emerge, with elements such as social/emotional learning that were previously missing. We are seeing teachers who have moved from being content deliverers to being project coaches. We are seeing technology being used to do new and powerful things. We are seeing organizations outside of schools emerge, such as Ashoka, that encourage kids to become "Changemakers."[17] We are hearing more and more kids say they want to change the world, and actually going out and doing so—not necessarily immensely, but rather, as Internet pioneer Vint Cerf puts it, by "setting out every day to make life better for someone (regardless of how many)."[18]

The world of K–12 education is currently entering a transition period from academics to real, world-improving accomplishment, with both plans side-by-side for a time. But academic education is the past. Bettering Their World is the future of education. And as we all know, the future is arriving at an accelerating rate.

NEW ENDS, NEW MEANS, NEW SUPPORT

To summarize, the big differentiators between today's academic education and tomorrow's empowerment to Better Their World education are these:

- *New ends:* The "ends" of today's academic education are individual achievement, typically expressed as grades, scores and rankings. The ends of tomorrow's "Better Their World" education are improving the world, and in so doing, becoming good, effective, world-improving people.
- *New means:* The means of academic education are proscribed courses of study, completed successfully in some number and

sequence. The means of Better Their World education are real-world local and global projects, completed in teams, in ways that apply each student's passions and increase students' overall ability to accomplish effectively. We must help our kids recognize potentially solvable problems in their world, and make them addressable though real-world projects. With so many issues and opportunities in our world, such projects will never be in short supply. Some are already adding "problem seeking" to their curricula.

- *A New, Broader, Supporting Curriculum:* Academic education consists of carefully constructed curricula—mostly MESS-based—that provide, in a sequential order, knowledge and skills to be absorbed now to be used later. Better Their World education has a far wider, almost entirely skills-based curriculum in a "support as needed" role, consisting of all the component skills that make up the needed-by-all abilities of Effective Thinking, Effective Action, Effective Relationships that lead, with application, to Effective Accomplishment These can be seen in Figure 9.1, in Chapter 9 of this book. These abilities are acquired not in sequence, but from peers, teachers, curated applications and the Internet, as needed, in order to accomplish projects.

- *New teaching*: In our academic K–12 education, teachers are primarily "content deliverers." In Better Their World education, teachers are "empowerers" and coaches, whose job is to guide students to get better and better at applying their unique personal passions and interests to effective, real-world accomplishment and, in the process, acquire a wide variety of essential thinking, action, and relationship skills.

THE REAL-WORLD PROJECTS

An important element of Better Their World education is identifying real-world problems and creating and connecting student teams to solve them—with adult (e.g., teacher) coaching and guidance. This requires that there be a constant supply of real-world projects at every level and in a wide variety of areas. Finding such projects and connecting student teams to them may once have been a daunting or impossible task, but it is fast becoming less challenging with today's technology.

Since I (and possibly others) are already working to create this, we will soon see one or more global databases of real-world projects already completed by students—in the areas of government, environment, technology, peer-to-peer help, historical preservation, etc.—along with a place for individuals, teachers, companies, and governments to input new project ideas. The kinds of mechanisms that would allow companies, governments, and others to propose problems for students to solve and to match students' interests to those problems already exist in the online world—in marketplace sites like eBay and Craigslist, job-matching sites like Monster and CareerBuilder, and people-matching sites such as Match and eHarmony—they will need only to be repurposed. An early prototype of how this might eventually look can be found at globalempoweredkids.org.

The world is replete with problems to be solved—we need create only a methodology for kids to identify and address them. Because "PBL" (project-based or problem-based learning) and related methodologies such as Apple's "challenge-based learning" have now been around for some time, and many teachers are familiar with them, we are already well down the project methodology path—although regrettably, we are still not using most of the power of such projects to improve the real world. But the development of PBL and its cousins has made the next crucial step of moving from the fake, made-up problems of most of today's project-based approaches to real-world problems far easier.

Once the databases and methodologies are in place, the next step is to create a mechanism to help students identify their personal passions and strengths, and, additionally, a dedicated recommendation engine— something we are already good at creating—to connect students to projects and roles of appropriate scope and level to help them advance. Such projects are already under development.[19]

THE BENEFITS

Imagine if kids, after leaving school, entered a university or job recruiter's office not as they do today—that is, with a transcript of grades and (at best) a vague idea of what they would like to accomplish—but rather, with an actual résumé of accomplishments. Such a résumé might include scores of projects completed over a K–12 career, in multiple areas and roles, and with a clear idea of the kinds of roles and projects that suit them best and excite their passion. This alone would be a reason to change to a Better Their World education. But we can add to that the benefits of thousands or millions of world-improving projects that are actually completed during the K–12 years—projects that would be adding, potentially, billions of dollars of value to the world.

HOW TO GET THERE—BUILDING THE DETAILED ROAD MAP(S)

The broad outline and map of an Education to Better Their World is clear, but the details still need to be worked out and adapted to the highly diverse individual situations around the world. Individual school systems, schools, and teachers will need to figure out how to do real-world accomplishment in ways that work for their local students and communities—bearing in mind, as they do, that their students, and the world, are all now connected. We can all help each other in this process—using our and our kids' connectivity, as well as the global databases and other tools already emerging. And in our evolution to a Better Their World eduction we must be sure, at every stage, to utilize and rely on our young people to help us. Education, in our new age, is no longer a top-down process, but rather a far stronger combination of top-down and bottom-up.

To make that happen, what is needed now more than anything is a change in mindset on the part of educators, parents, politicians, and other adults. What is required is a realization by everyone that our academic education—despite the fact that it got all of us adults us to the place we are—is no longer right for our kids or for the future. The time has come for something new and better. Those who maintain their allegiance only to an academic education, and who devote their funds and efforts only to improving academic education incrementally—whether through technology, 21st century skills, STEM (science, technology, engineering, mathematics), STEAM (the same with arts), or anything else besides real-world projects—do so in vain, and are bound long-term to fail.

OUR EDUCATION MUST SUPPORT OUR STUDENTS—AND THE FUTURE

We have a new generation of empowered kids in the world and the only trend worth supporting is one that further empowers them in the future. Our choice is either to accelerate this trend and guide it in the positive direction most of us (particularly the kids) want, or to stand in its way and continue to tweak an expiring system. The map to Better Their World education is already clear—its **new ends** of world improvement, its **new means** of real-world accomplishment, its **new, supporting curriculum** of effective thinking, effective action, effective relationships, and effective accomplishment with young people acquiring those abilities not *before* doing, but *through* doing real-world projects, and its **new teaching role** of coaching and empowering rather than delivering content.

This new education will not come into all our schools immediately—it will be a gradual, though accelerating process. But any school or class that currently offers *only* academic education is failing its students, no matter how many bells and whistles—from iPads, to critical thinking seminars, to Mandarin—it may be adding to its programs. Schools in places like Finland, and start-ups like AltSchool and Summit Public Schools in the United States are already moving to mixed plans with, for example, academic classes in the morning and real, world-improving projects in the afternoon. Schools with long-standing "service projects" are adding more of them and granting them more importance. Former "capstone" projects are becoming the actual building stones of an education.

The era of the academic model of education—learn first, achieve later—is ending. It may have been useful in the past, but learning *before* doing no longer works, and that is no longer the education our kids want and need. Today, more and more people—both kids and adults—are realizing that we must move to something new. Our goal must be to help all of our people become world-class accomplishers at whatever they are interested in, passionate about, and good at.

It's now time to make it happen, universally.

CHAPTER 7

What Kids Could Accomplish
The Value Kids Can Add by Applying their Passions to Real, World-Improving Projects

IN ALL OUR DISCUSSIONS for and against technology in education, one of the biggest and most obvious benefits is being almost completely overlooked—technology's empowering of our youth to accomplish huge amounts of desperately needed tasks in the world.

Perhaps this is because in the past, before modern technology, kids really couldn't accomplish much until they were older. Perhaps it is because we are conditioned by our pre-Internet past against exploitative child labor. Or, perhaps it is because for so long we have kept our young people from accomplishing anything we have forgotten what they are capable of.

But now, a great deal has changed. Half the people on the planet are under the age of 25, and they are increasingly, individually and as a group, hugely capable and powerful—and linked to each other in ways that never existed before.

Until we liberate our young people to accomplish for the world all the positive things they now can, we are wasting half the world's capability—just as for a long time we wasted much of the capability of women.

Not only can today's youth, often with the help of technology, accomplish much that is truly useful in the world, and in the places they live, but in the process of doing so they will grow into precisely the kind of people we want. Some of this accomplishment and growth will likely happen whether we act, or not—many kids have already started on their own. But if we help our young people to accomplish, rather than hold them back, the process will go much faster.

In the past it was assumed—mostly correctly—that students could not compete with adults for work. We expected our young people to learn first and earn later. Doing it the other way was scorned as either exploitation or "dropping out."

But those beliefs, like most of the beliefs and attitudes of today's adults, were formed in pre-Internet times. Today, kids are fast becoming far more capable, and this is true everywhere. "Millennials worldwide are more similar to one another than to older generations within their nations," wrote *Time* magazine in 2014.

Today, many adults are dismayed to see elements of their local cultures fading as their kids grow up in a new global world. Many are afraid of the generation that is now growing up, and of their own children. They worry about what they perceive as negative behavior, such as young people communicating through screens rather than face to face. But their fear, unfortunately, also blinds them to the positive side of how much power these young people have to do good for the world.

In today's Internet world, not only can young people compete with adults in many areas, but they can often do the work better, as people in more and more fields are finding out to their dismay. Even today's primary school students can build professional websites.

Our young people are starting early and are flocking especially to the world's newer jobs, such as search engine optimization and social media strategy. It would be a mistake to see the few well-known individuals who have started billion-dollar companies in their dorm rooms as exceptions in their essence—they are exceptional only in the magnitude of their accomplishments. All today's kids are totally capable of accomplishing real things during the years that we used to think were only about "learning."

NOT GRADES—ACCOMPLISHMENTS

Today, when school administrators want to demonstrate what they are doing right, they increasingly point not to test scores, but to accomplishments of their individual students and groups of students in the world. You can watch a video of them doing this at www.dcsdk12.org/community-relations/job-alike-robotic-students.

Huge numbers of such student accomplishments exist. They are sometimes referred to as "volunteer opportunities" or "impact education." At the moment, they are often done outside of school. One can find such opportunities listed on a great many websites such as, for example, www.lancaster.unl.edu/4h/serviceideas.shtml and www.dillerteenawards.org/past-recipients/.

Here are 10 examples, copied directly (with permission) from the website www.teenlife.com:

1. Jonathan Woods established the Under the Tree foundation aged 12, when he realized that teens are often overlooked during toy drives.
2. Neha Gupta began her nonprofit at the age of nine! Her organization, Empower Orphans, has helped more than 25,000 children globally.
3. Jordyn Schara founded WI P2D2 (Wisconsin Prescription Pill and Drug Disposal), which works to dispose of drugs in an environmentally friendly and safe way, when she turned 14.
4. 10-year-old Zach Certner started his organization, SNAP, as an athletic program for children with special needs.
5. Shannon McNamara started SHARE, a nonprofit that provides thousands of girls in Africa with books and school supplies, when she was 15 years old.
6. Kalin Konrad started her annual backyard carnival for Alzheimer's when she was in fifth grade. Kalin originally began the event when her grandmother was diagnosed with the disease.
7. 13-year-old Claire Fraise wanted to give dogs who would be euthanized a second chance with her organization, Lucky Tails Animal Rescue.
8. Former anorexic teens Liana Rosenman and Kristina Saffran decided to start Project HEAL to raise money for teens who needed treatment for eating disorders.
9. LuLu Cerone founded LemonAID Warriors at 10 years old to help other kids make social activism part of their lives.
10. Wanting to end hunger, Katie Stagliano, now 14, started planting fruits and vegetables in her garden to help the hungry. Her organization, Katie's Krops, has helped feed thousands of people so far. [20]

At the moment, most of these real-world accomplishments by students are isolated, unconnected, and outside of the educational mainstream. They are often done in the context of after-school activities such as 4H (a long time after-school youth development program in the U.S.) and scouting. Yet, in actuality, this is the most important part of our children's education. In doing these projects, kids learn whatever skills they need to "get things done" and typically much more. They also develop something that school rarely provides—a real sense of accomplishment in the world. Not in the school world, but in the real world.

If the goal of education is for our children to become better, more effective people, who improve the world and are well-prepared for their future, "accomplishing" is a far better means to that goal than is the "learning" on which almost all our schools are fixated today. Very little of our current curriculum prepares our students for real-world accomplishment. Our students are realizing increasingly that they can in many cases prepare themselves better for the future on their own than by the education we currently offer them.

THE NEED FOR "REAL"

Many educators have finally realized that just learning content, however well, does not make kids into better, more effective people. Many places have moved to skill-based education (e.g., the U.S.'s Common Core), and others have added problem-based, inquiry-based, and project-based learning to their curricula. But while this is in some ways a step in the right direction, it misses something truly basic: almost none of it is "real."

Almost all of our school problems and activities are "made up," designed to include the maximum number of learnings or standards. They are *not* designed to accomplish anything useful in the world. What we need instead is an education where the outcomes make a difference, and provide real improvements to the world. This is what I call a real "world-improving accomplishment–based education.

The students I talk to around the world are crying out for this kind of real-world education. Raised in large part on the Internet, games and social media, they are far better at both cooperation and competition than we ever were. They know their power and capabilities, and are frustrated at not being given the chance, daily, to use them. When they focus on tasks they are truly interested in and passionate about, the amount of enthusiasm, energy, and intellect that they put forth is prodigious.

Real-world accomplishment-based education is certainly not a wholly new idea—there are students around the world already devoting large chunks of their energy to real problems. Educator Zoe Weil[1] has even coined a term for these people: "Solutionaries."

The issue, rather, is that this kind of education is almost completely haphazard, scattered, and random in the world, depending on, and limited to, individual teachers, administrators, and schools. We can and should help organize this to a much greater extent for all our students. For example:

- We moan, in many places, about the sorry state of our network infrastructure and connections. Our young people are totally capable of fixing this—most of the instructions already can be found on the Internet.
- We hold science, robotics, and other competitions that are marvels of student creativity and enthusiasm. But too often teams compete only to shoot balls through hoops or to demonstrate something they have learned. Why can't they be competing to drill water wells, clean up dumps, put out fires, or to do other useful tasks?
- Where physical infrastructure doesn't exist (e.g., in villages that lack clean water) or is crumbling (e.g., throughout the United States), students could be doing much of the work of designing, planning, funding, and even fixing or building the infrastructure; putting the necessary steps and procedures online is trivial. Often, adults are needed only to keep students from breaking laws or hurting themselves.

So why can't this kind of real-world accomplishing *be* our education? How hard would it be to put together, as a start, all the examples in the world of kids doing real projects during or as part of their school years? How simple would it be, using these projects as examples, to build upon that base in every school and classroom? How complex would it be to compile a list of needed accomplishments in places, and let students choose the ones that interest them? For how long must our education remain artificial preparation for accomplishment, rather than accomplishment itself?

Whatever issues there might be, such as children taking adults' jobs, or compensation for their work, or other things, we can and must work through them. Because if we don't do this in partnership with our kids, they will only go around us and do it themselves.

Real-world accomplishment-based education is something we can—and must—do. And, hopefully do it soon.

WHAT KIDS CAN ACCOMPLISH: APPLIED PASSION, REAL, WORLD-IMPROVING PROJECTS, AND THE VALUE KIDS CAN ADD

Just how much could our kids accomplish if we set them free? How much value could they add to the world? The answer is a function of two things: How much passion our kids have, and how they—with adults' help—are able to apply it.

THE IMPORTANCE OF PASSION, AND OF EVERY STUDENT FINDING IT

Kids' passion, when found, is unbounded, and there is almost nothing more important a K–12 education can do for a kid than to help him or her find and recognize whatever passion they have at that point in their life. If we did nothing more than help every kid understand what his or her passion is by the end of their K–12 years, our education would be far better than it is today. A big reason for this is that higher education works incredibly better for kids who go in to it already knowing what they want to do.

The kind of passion that stems from kids' interests is also a key factor in success in life—particularly when combined with other things like persistence and skill development. Student passion has recently been getting more attention in educational circles, and educator interest in helping students identify their own passion appears to be increasing—the term "passion-based education" (or learning) is now on many people's lips and in many people's writings.[21]

The reason that finding passion is key to truly educating kids is that *passion motivates people*, independent of what anyone tells them they can or can't, or should or shouldn't do. Almost everyone is passionate about something, although at times one may have to dig deep to find out what it is.

It should also be noted that "student passion" is hardly restricted to the school curriculum. In fact, while most educators would love for all their kids to become passionate about the MESS and the rest of the current curriculum, not all do. What students really need—and want—is to be able to find their passion—whatever it may be—and apply it to tasks that they, and we, consider worthwhile and world-improving.

APPLIED PASSION

As important as passion is, passion that is not *applied*—and carefully applied, using the many tools invented over the ages—can easily be wasted. A hugely important job of education is to help kids not only find their passion, but to apply it effectively to something real and useful.

Helping kids identify their own passions and strengths, and then apply them, are things that we—as a society and as educators—now do particularly poorly. We do an even less satisfactory job of connecting the passions and interests of those who *do* find them to a wide variety of possible careers.

But we can, and should, do much better. I have long maintained that the most helpful thing that any teacher can do for all students— without even much effort—is to go around the classroom and ask each student, "What are you passionate about?" (And then, importantly, write it down so they can later reflect on how that student can best apply it and how they can use the information in their teaching.)

WHAT IF KIDS DON'T KNOW?

"But many of my kids don't know what their passion is" is a response I often hear from teachers. A common mistake that adults—not just teachers—often make is to think that when they ask kids, "What are you passionate about?" and the kids respond with a shrug, that the kids really don't have a passion deep down. All kids, I believe, have passion for something—it is part of being human. The trick is to know how to probe and help each kid uncover what their passion is—something many teachers (and parents) may not feel they have the time or skill to do. But, for our kids' sake, we must get better at it.

I've also heard teachers say when asked about their students' passions, "All my kids just want to be rock stars, or sports stars." To me, this indicates a misunderstanding of the distinction between aspiration, or desire, and true passion. Passion, as we talk about it in the context of education, is *intense interest in something that will make a kid work hard of his or her own volition*. While certainly few of our kids will achieve true stardom, we must help these kids understand that this is different from what they are passionate about. If kids are truly passionate about music or sports and want to be part of those worlds, there are a huge variety of options depending on their strengths—from performer, to manager, coach, publicist, and more. (There are over 300 people employed by a professional basketball team, for example, of whom only 12 actually play basketball.) When kids' passion is truly for making money, we can steer them into entrepreneurship and particular careers.

When asked about their passion, many kids respond that they "don't know" because they believe, when a teacher asks, that the answer has to be something related to school. Sadly, we do much to encourage this. Rather than asking our kids the more helpful question of, "What are your interests?" we too often ask them, "What is your favorite subject?" as if those were the only choices. Although some kids may have a deep passion for what we teach in school, certainly a great many do not.

It would also be a mistake to misattribute a perceived lack of passion on the part of students to a so-called lack of "exposure." More exposure to, and learning more about other areas may cause kids' passions to expand or change, but it won't change the likelihood of their having one or more of them. I deeply believe, based on every kid I have ever met, that passion and the desire to apply it is something every kid has, or can have. Some people become clear on what their passion is early on in their lives; in others it may come later, and it is certainly changeable many times over the course of a lifetime. But knowing your own passion is so important that it is worth a great deal of effort for every kid to find, and worth a great deal of our effort as educators to help each of our kids find.

My approach, whenever I try to help kids uncover their passions, is to ask them the following kinds of questions:

- When you are by yourself, what is your favorite thing you like to do with your time? Why?
- If you could subscribe to a YouTube channel about only one thing, what would it be? Why?
- What or who is something or someone you care a lot about. Why?
- Do you notice any particular problems in the world around you? Which ones?
- If you had the power, what in your community or life would you fix or change? How?

PASSION SEEKERS AND EVOLVING PASSION

There are, of course, some kids who are *truly* not able to say at any given time what their passion is. My preferred designation for these people is "passion seekers." Calling people—kids or adults—by that name helps them understand that there is something inside them that they should be looking for.

It is also possible for a student or an adult to have more than one passion, and it is uncommon for someone to remain passionate about the same thing or things for their entire life. Passions evolve and change with life experiences, and kids should know that they are not constrained to the same interests they have now for the rest of their lives. Kids should be encouraged to be on the lookout for and be aware of new passions developing within themselves as a result of new experiences. But it is often the case that passions kids have early in life are what they really love to do.

LEARNING ABOUT ONE'S PASSION IS GREAT . . .

It is almost always enjoyable for kids to learn more about whatever they are passionate about. Once they are aware of their passions, such learning typically takes little effort on the part of students or teachers—it is something that kids are happy to do on their own. The adults' role is mostly a matter of providing encouragement and guidance. A practical way to encourage kids to learn more about what they are passionate about is to have them keep a "passion journal," either in written form or electronically (through, for example, video recording and voice-to-text apps available on many kids' phones). This can also be done through apps like Pinterest, and by encouraging kids to make and post YouTube videos, sharing what they have learned with others.

. . . BUT IT'S APPLYING THEIR PASSION TO REAL-WORLD PROJECTS THAT COUNTS

But our kids need to know that learning about whatever they are passionate about is only the start, not the end. It is crucial that all kids and adults understand that just recognizing and knowing your passion (whether lifelong or of the moment) is the very beginning of an important process. Once a person knows what his or her passion is, their goal must be to apply it, because it is *applied passion* that really counts.

All kids have to figure out—and we have to help them figure out—ways to apply their passion through real-world accomplishment. This goes way beyond "learning by doing." Kids are typically far more motivated, and gain far more self-confidence, when accomplishing something that is of value not just to them, but to others. So we must help kids find and accomplish real-world projects that apply their passion to bettering their world.

In academic education, unless your passion happens to coincide with something in the MESS, you typically don't get to use it. And, more importantly, whether it coincides or not, you almost never get to apply it to something real. In fact, in academic education the designated place to apply your passion is *outside* of your formal classroom education, in an extracurricular activity—almost always accorded lesser value than the MESS itself. If your passion is science, there are science fairs. If your passion is sports, or even chess, there are typically teams. But if your passion happens to be for something minor or exotic (say, rare coins or longboarding), to get any kind of school support there needs to be both enough students in your school interested *and* a sponsor available in order for it to be squeezed into an extracurricular club.

So in order to learn more about and apply their passion, more and more kids today, are forced to go completely outside of school, either onto the Internet (which is great for uniting widely scattered people with obscure interests), or into various after-school programs. There is a long tradition of service organizations like Scouts, 4H, and other groups around the world doing some of this. LRNG[22], a recent startup, aims to help kids more easily apply their passions after school while hanging out in libraries and other places.

TODAY, APPLYING PASSION COMES TOO LATE IN EDUCATION

In today's academic education, the priority is very clear: you learn first, and you apply—especially to the real world—later (most likely after you have proved, mostly through testing, that you are ready). Even the growing PBL movement does not have much real-world accomplishment—at least not yet. Those academic programs that do include real-world accomplishment (and some do) typically put it at the end of the learning process as a capstone, or a performance, or a service project.

K–12 is, at its core, a place to learn the standard MESS-based curriculum. Unless a students' passion is MESS-based (or in some places for a mainstream sport), it is considered at best secondary, and often irrelevant. Applying passion is something kids do elsewhere—in the same way adults with jobs they don't like find outside hobbies they are passionate about.

THE ALTERNATIVE

But there's another option. Suppose, for example, that a school year consisted *entirely* of projects, undertaken continuously by groups—either classes, small teams, or larger and/or technology-enabled teams. Suppose we found better ways to help students identify their passions and to apply them to these real-world projects in a variety of roles. Suppose that we found a way to help kids choose projects, and roles that both the kids and their teachers thought would stretch them in positive directions.

And suppose that, as they did these projects, we found ways to be sure that the projects included not just "learning about" but *actually using* effective thinking, effective action, and effective relationships on the part of the teams and kids. That would go a long way to applying kids' passions in useful ways.

For this to happen widely, we need to do three things:

1. Create an effective system for enabling kids to do real-world projects and for evaluating them;
2. Share a full sense of what the subjects, breadth, and goals of these projects would and could be; and
3. Connect students with appropriate projects that they will be passionate about.

The first of these—i.e., the process of helping kids structure and accomplish real-world projects and of evaluating kids' accomplishment within these projects—has already begun. The PBL movement and its related cousins—including challenges, capstones, competitions, and science fairs, are often far from real-world, but they have nonetheless taught us much about, and have established good models for doing, project-based work. The challenge now is to make all of our projects real-world. As we do this we will discover—happily, I believe—that evaluating accomplishment, is easier and more useful than struggling to evaluate learning.

FINDING AND CREATING GOOD PROJECTS

If finding enough useful real-world projects for kids to choose from and do—the second need—were made easier, it would be of enormous help. One huge step forward would be a database of potential projects in the world. Such a database, if it existed, would contain all the real-world projects ever undertaken and accomplished by students around the world (so that they could be redone in new contexts), as well as suggested projects students could accomplish, plus ways for people to enter the projects that kids could do. Projects would need to be searchable along several dimensions, including subject area, role, age-appropriateness, possible prerequisite skills and experience, and other criteria. It's my fervent goal to see such a database be created in the world.

CATEGORIES OF REAL-WORLD PROJECTS

Having searched for such projects, and having attempted to create the rudiments of such a database, I have seen projects falling into particular categories. A partial listing would include:

- Projects to help your local physical community, e.g.
  - » Cleaning up areas
  - » Creating local parks and gardens
  - » Designing local amenities
- Projects to help the less fortunate, e.g.
  - » Redistributing discarded material
  - » Connecting with seniors
  - » Creating technology to assist them
- Projects to help build and repair infrastructure, e.g.
  - » Digging wells
  - » Building water cisterns
  - » Improving sanitation
  - » Putting in Wi-Fi and Internet connections

- Projects to directly assist peers or others, e.g.
  - » Tutoring
  - » Connecting with seniors
- Projects to help preserve our history and legacy, e.g.
  - » Restoring community artifacts (such as wooden boats)
  - » Digitizing texts
- Projects to assist with government functions, e.g.
  - » Measuring air and water quality
  - » Creating required reports
- Projects adding new information to the world's knowledge and databases, e.g.
  - » Citizen science
  - » Invention and innovation
- Projects for public service, e.g.
  - » Evaluating public services and personnel

While these are far from all the possible categories for student projects, seeing these categories may be useful in helping kids, and others, think of and find additional world-improving projects to do. Students, in collaboration with their teachers, should be thinking up not just more and more projects, but more and more *categories* of projects. To see examples in several of the categories mentioned above, please go to www.globalempowerdkids.org.

CONNECTING STUDENTS WITH PROJECTS

The third need—devising ways of connecting kids to projects that allow them to both apply their passions and stretch their abilities—is an area where a lot more effort would be helpful—it is a place where investment will really pay huge benefits. Today, we rely mostly on the judgment of our kids and teachers (and when available councilors) to do this, but all of them lack considerable information about both what our kids' passions are and what the project possibilities are at any given time. So in addition to the database I spoke of, it would be really useful to have more ways—technology-based and otherwise—to help kids identify their passions and to connect those directly to suggestions for projects from the database. We already know how to make such connections through the "recommendation engines" created by Amazon and others, so doing this would be very feasible. Encouraging more of this kind of software to be developed for education is another big objective of mine.

NOT JUST WRITING REPORTS OR COLLECTING DONATIONS

It is also crucial, as we noted earlier, for people to understand just what real, world-improving projects are—and particularly what they are not. What is meant by real, world-improving projects are projects that students select themselves, and do typically in teams, that produce actual (and hopefully lasting) changes in their local and global communities—changes that they can point to and say, "I, with my team, did that!"

Projects that are *not* real-world include students doing research that leads to a report or to recommendations (even if the recommendations or report do get submitted to some official group). A project is real-world *only* if it leads to action and a difference. Writing a letter to a politician is not by itself a real, world-improving project, although lobbying that actually leads to legislation—as in the case of the 16-year-old Illinois girl whose project led to a statewide ban on plastic bags—is.[23]

Also *not* included in the category of real, world-improving projects are the many so-called projects that students do involving raising money for particular causes. These are admirable, and kids may benefit from being involved with them. But fund-raising projects alone are not the kind of real, world-improving projects I am talking about. The kids need to cause the world improvements themselves, through their own efforts, rather than by helping fund someone else to do it.

RECOGNIZING THE VALUE THAT IS ADDED, THROUGH PAY OR IMPUTED PAY—CHILD LABOR 2.0?

Should students who add real value through world-improving projects be paid for this work? That is a question that proponents of Better Their World education will have to address, as these kinds of new, non-exploitive student projects become more widespread and an integral part of the education and development process of our kids. An important thing kids generally don't learn in school today is exactly what their own work—and other people's work—is worth. How should kids be compensated for value that they are able to add?

If, for example, a school team does a project that a local government formerly paid consultants $50,000 to do, where does that value go? Does some of it go to the school? Does some of it go to the kids? Does some of it go into escrow for some future purpose? Or does it get captured in the fact that government, through its education arm, is now more efficient? A hugely valuable development would be to find a way to impute value to projects, even if no actual money exchanges hands.

Already, companies are employing school-age kids directly, outside of school, to build websites, collect data, and do other tasks they typically pay for. What if the kids start doing this in school? When kids start successful for-profit companies by themselves, inside or outside of school, such as on the Internet, what protections should be given to their intellectual property? Perhaps student compensation can be done through some version of "badging" or "credits," or through a process of negotiation that mimics—and helps students understand—what goes on in the real world.

Along with this comes the issue of kids' understanding how to maximize the value of what they individually and uniquely bring to the world, both in financial and nonfinancial terms. Do we want our kids to see directly, and early on, that the world pays much more for some kinds of work and projects than for others, and that the value of an hour of work depends enormously on what that work is, and even where it is done? Should our kids be learning, through their projects, how to apply their passions and skills in the most lucrative directions? Should schools, at the extreme, be rated on the value their students can create, value measured either financially or in some other way?

I do not have answers to these questions. But in view of our kids' new capabilities and our quest for equity and meritocracy in the world, these are all important issues worth making part of our educational discussions.

CHAPTER 8

Achievement vs. Accomplishment

WE HAVE SPENT much time considering real-world accomplishment, but schools and parents are often concerned with student achievement. Are "achievement" and "accomplishment" the same thing?

Many use the terms interchangeably. A student who earns high marks is "achieving," and we might say that getting a PhD, or even getting through a particular course, or year, is "quite an accomplishment." But I suggest that we put a finer point on it, because there is an important distinction to be made here—whatever words we use to make it.

The distinction I suggest we make when thinking about accomplishment-based education is between a person's doing something that benefits only (or principally) him or her (= an achievement), versus a person's doing something (or being part of doing something) that benefits others and the world outside of that person (= an accomplishment).

Climbing to the top of Mount Everest, for example, is an achievement. Climbing a mountain "because it's there" as many say, benefits no one but the climber. And often it leaves the world with a trail of debris—and even dead companions. Winning a race is an achievement, but it typically benefits only the winner.

In education, obtaining a 4.0 average, or high marks in an exam, or a special prize, are achievements. Getting elected to school office is an achievement. In fact, most of what we expect from our students today is achievement. Achievement takes effort, often a great deal of it. And that effort, if positive, should be celebrated. We should laud the achievements of our students, teachers, and others.

ACCOMPLISHMENT

But these achievements are quite different from *accomplishment*, at least in this context. Winning a race, or getting good grades, or getting to the top of a mountain, are achievements but *not* accomplishments as I use the word here. This is because those things benefit no one but the person who did them. Accomplishments benefit others and the real world.

Helping find a cure for a disease is an accomplishment. Getting that cure into the field and eliminating the disease is an even bigger accomplishment. Starting (or contributing to) a magazine that becomes influential is an accomplishment. Starting a successful company that does something useful is an accomplishment. Helping improve your neighborhood is an accomplishment.

Even the highest achievements are not necessarily accomplishments and we shouldn't, I believe, alternatively describe them as such (despite the fact that in ordinary language we often do). I believe we should reserve the word accomplishment for things we do that help the world, or part of it. We achieve, in fact, so that we *can* accomplish.

School kids may collect achievements. But our students typically have far fewer accomplishments. This is because so little of what kids do in school do affects the real world. But our students could — and should — be accomplishing as well.

Writing a report that is accepted by the government in place of the one consultants used to be paid to do—as happened with the sixth-grade class referenced earlier—is an accomplishment that is far better than the achievement of getting an "A" grade on a paper on the environment. Getting a team's design for a community water park approved by the local board and built—as that fifth grade class did—is an accomplishment far beyond the achievement of creating a good or winning design.

Accomplishments are things that go in the "experience" section of the résumé, beyond where you went to school, what your grades were, and what extracurricular activities you undertook.

WHY THE DISTINCTION MATTERS IN EDUCATION

The distinction between achievement and accomplishment is important in education because "high achievers" in school, unfortunately, often accomplish little—many studies show that grades are a terrible predictor of success in life. And, at the same time, there are many people who accomplish a great deal for the world but were never high achievers in the academic sense. Winston Churchill is a great example.

What we really want from our students, I believe, is accomplishment and not achievement. We want them not only to understand the distinction between achievement and accomplishment, and what an accomplishment really is, but to accomplish, over and over, as many times as they can during their school years—so that they will know they *can* accomplish things in the real world, and how good it makes them feel. "Nothing builds self-esteem and self-confidence like accomplishment," writes the Scottish philosopher Thomas Carlyle.

Today, some schools require real-world service or capstone projects as a (generally small) part of their programs. These can and should be expanded to the entire curriculum. Our young people should be working to build in school a résumé of accomplishments and not just achievements.

Were we and our schools to measure student accomplishment (i.e., the positive value of projects a student has had an important hand in getting done) rather than student achievement (how high a grade or rank each student can get), the perceptions we have of our students—and our education—would likely be quite different. So I suggest that, as the new educational model and paradigm emerges, we all begin to distinguish more carefully between achievement and accomplishment in our education, and in our kids. We will all be better off.

CHAPTER 9

All the Skills Kids Need
A Far Broader Supporting Curriculum—Acquired Differently

IN THE EMERGING Better Their World Paradigm, the means through which K–12 education is delivered is real, world-improving projects. But what, in this new model of education, supports those projects?

Remember, the ends of Better Their World education are to improve the world *and,* for our kids to become-though the process of doing and completing projects that do so—good, effective, world-improving people. So, our kids have to acquire through the Better Their World education process not just the knowledge and skills required to do each project, but a lifelong set of skills and dispositions that *makes* them good, effective, and world-improving people.

So we must therefore ask: "In addition to having accomplished—and knowing, therefore, that they *can* accomplish—and having lots of real-world accomplishments on their résumés, *what else* do we want all our kids to have acquired as a result of their roughly dozen years of primary, elementary, and secondary education? What—in this increasingly technology and artificial-intelligence-filled world our kids now live in—is still important for all humans to acquire and become better at?" Our answer to that question becomes our curriculum. And once we have established that curriculum, we must figure out how to deliver it.

OUT WITH THE MESS: RETHINKING THE CURRICULUM'S "BASICS"

Even when confronted with huge contextual changes and the need for educational changes to meet and address them, most adults opine that our kids "still need the basics." I do agree that there are roots that are important to put in place in the early years so that kids can continue to grow and thrive.

But what is crucial to understand is that *basics are context-dependent;* they change when the context shifts. For an amusing and instructive example of this, in the form of a short parody and fable, I highly recommend that readers check out *The Saber-Tooth Curriculum* at www. bit.ly/1OqGlSD.[24]

What "the basics" will be in our future times is a question that is not asked or addressed frequently enough.

Today, in our universal academic education, the world sees the basics as, essentially, getting all our kids to go as far as they are able in four subject areas: math, language arts (which includes reading and writing, and to which many countries add a second language), science, and social studies. Since its modern codification in the late 19th century, these four basic subjects have come to dominate the K–12 world. All our teachers are specialists in instructing kids in one of these four areas (and our primary teachers are supposed to do all of them.) We ask our kids, "What is your favorite subject?" as if there were only four choices.

Although today most recognize that the context in which our education is situated has changed or is changing, people typically look only to accretion—i.e., to "adding on" to what we have—rather than looking to replace our old basics with new ones.

As mentioned earlier, I often refer to our current quadrivium of basic subjects as the MESS, after its acronym in the English-speaking world (**M**ath, **E**nglish, **S**cience, and **S**ocial studies). No one picks up on the term MESS faster than the kids. It's pretty much how they see it, and with good reason.

Because we've been teaching these same four core subjects of math, language arts, science, and social studies universally for so long, many have come to accept the false notion that those four topics are what education is truly about. (That is why, for example, people will actually believe and accept that a narrowly focused test, such as the Program for International Student Assessment (PISA), can compare and rank "education" in countries across the world.)

The MESS, of course, has served many of us well—and various elements of the MESS are, and will always be, useful to individual students. But I strongly believe that the MESS is one of the biggest impediments to moving toward a more effective education for our kids. Key reasons include that:

- the MESS narrows our curriculum tremendously and unnecessarily, leaving out huge numbers of important skills;

- the MESS subjects are not of equal importance to everyone;
- we treat the four MESS subjects in far too much detail;
- even when we combine the MESS subjects by being interdisciplinary and theme-focused it is not enough, because the MESS includes little, if anything, about the important areas of Effective Action, Relationships, and Accomplishment.

It's time for the MESS, as most of the world conceives of and teaches it today, to go away as the basics, or core, of our K–12 curriculum.

Somehow, today, we have gotten things backwards. Not only is most of what we teach *not* necessary for *all* students, but most of the things that *are* essential for all students are not a part, in any systematic way, of their K–12 education. The need for math, language, science, and social studies skills will continue to be important for many. But the MESS is a poor candidate for the core structure and organization of tomorrow's curriculum, and "tweaks" won't fix it. Neither interdisciplinary and team-teaching approaches, "big themes," questions of global importance, increased rigor (e.g., the Common Core initiative in the United States), nor so-called 21st-century skills (such as entrepreneurship and the 4 "Cs" of communication, creativity, collaboration, and critical thinking) go far enough to do the job.

For our curriculum to truly support the new ends of empowering kids to better their world, and the new means of real-world accomplishment, our future curriculum needs to go much farther, and completely rethink what the basics of a K–12 education are. In doing so, we can bring the two traditions we spoke of earlier—the thinking tradition and the accomplishing tradition—into a new unified whole that truly supports students in improving their world, and improving themselves through that process.

"NEW BASICS"

Were we to abandon the MESS, though, with what would we replace it? What *are* the basics—leaving aside all our establishment and tradition—that our kids really need? What skills should everyone acquire? Were we to start from scratch, what would be the core of a curriculum that truly supports the ends of bettering our kids' world and of their becoming good, effective, world-improving people?

The answer, I believe, is the complete set of useful skills that humans have conceived, thought about, and used over the ages to improve the world. We'd like to be sure that *all* of these skills are transmitted to *all* our kids in their formative years, as part of their education. Not just a narrow band of them, and definitely not in excruciating detail as we now do with the MESS. But rather, as areas that every kid leaving school knows exist and knows are important, as topics that all our kids have some general knowledge about, and—most important—as skills that our kids have had the experience of applying to real-world projects and accomplishment. We might call these "basic success skills."

Looked at from that perspective, our basic success skills would certainly *not* be the MESS, which is perhaps why we have so much trouble getting our kids to accept the curriculum of today as being of much use to them.

A "BETTER" WORLD CURRICULUM

So what if instead of organizing our education at the top level by the four MESS subjects of math, language arts, science, and social studies and measuring and evaluating our kids only on them (e.g., "How good are you in math? What's your verbal SAT score?" "What is your country's PISA ranking in science?"), and perhaps tacking on to them a small number of 21st century or social/emotional skills, we chose an entirely different framework for our education?

Suppose we were to organize education—comprehensively from kindergarten to secondary—around four very different top-level subjects. What if we organized education around the skills that we want *all* our kids to leave school possessing—that is, the key skills that are *actually important to the success of every person in the world*?

I believe that if we did this, those four subjects would be the following:

- Effective Thinking
- Effective Action
- Effective Relationships
- Effective Accomplishment

Those are the top-level skills that people—anyone—needs to be good at in order to have a useful and successful life, no matter what their location, work, or interests. Those skills need to be applied, of course, in specific instances, which is what the projects are for. Accomplishing the projects is the primary means and focus of a Better Their World education. But along the way, it is also our job to ensure that a student considers and applies to the projects each of the components shown in Figure 9.1.

Figure 9.1

EFFECTIVE THINKING	EFFECTIVE ACTION	EFFECTIVE RELATIONSHIPS
Understanding Communication	Habits of Highly	Communication &
Quantitative & Pattern Thinking	Effective People	Collaboration
Scientific Thinking	Body & Health optimization	• One-to-one
Historical Perspective	Agility	• In teams
Problem-Solving	Adaptability	• In families
• Individual	Leadership & Followership	• In communities
• Collaborative	Decision Making	• At work
Curiosity & Questioning	Under Uncertainty	• Online
Creative Thinking	Experimentation	• In virtual worlds
Design Thinking	Research	Listening
Integrative Thinking	Prudent Risk-taking	Networking
Systems Thinking	Reality Testing/Feedback	Relationship-building
Financial Thinking	Patience	Empathy
Inquiry & Argument	Resilience & "Grit"	Courage
Judgment	Entrepreneurship	Compassion
Transfer	Innovation	Tolerance
Aesthetics	Improvisation	Ethics
Habits of Mind	Ingenuity	Politics
Growth Mindset	Strategy & Tactics	Citizenship
Self-knowledge of one's:	Breaking Barriers	Conflict Resolution
• Passions	Project Management	Negotiation
• Strengths & weaknesses	Programming Machines	Coaching
Stress Control	Making Effective Videos	Being Coached
Focus	Innovating with Current &	Peer-to-peer
Contemplation & Meditation	Future Technologies	Mentoring

I will expand in a moment on each of these three core areas and their components. The fourth area, Effective Accomplishment, consists of the real-world projects themselves—small or local projects and accomplishments in the early school years, and larger, eventually worldwide, projects and accomplishments in later years. The categories of projects, as we have seen, are extremely broad, and the choice of what projects each student accomplishes will depend on a combination of the student's interests and passions, the needs of the community and world, and the skills teachers feel it is in the best interest of each individual student to acquire or improve.

WHY "EFFECTIVE"?

In naming these new core subject areas—thinking, acting, relating, and accomplishing, I include the adjective "effective" for each. That adjective is there, for me, not as a definer ("effective" takes a huge variety of different forms), but rather to distinguish it from "ineffective." Most of us have learned to recognize the distinction between effective and ineffective, although it's often difficult. Our young people need, as part of their education, as much practice as we can give them in making this distinction.

We can readily see by examining the above list that most of the topics in it are not covered, either systematically or at all, in most schools. It's also worth noting that *all* of the so-called 21st century skills so far proposed, and other proposed frameworks (such as the so-called 4Cs of communication, collaboration, creativity, and critical thinking) comprise only a small fraction of the skills kids need to learn in order to be successful.

NOT COURSES OR CLASSES

In the Better Their World model, unlike in an academic education, *none* of the listed topics—all of which are hugely important—would be taught in traditional classes with a scope, sequence, and prescribed level of detail as our curricula are typically taught today. Instead, the key elements of each of these topics would be available online, as needed, in video, animation, text and other formats, at various levels. This will require a big rethinking of each of these topics, as well as a major redesign of whatever curricula already exist, to be more "just-in-time." We do not yet have these topics organized and available in the way we need, but it would be a worthwhile effort to create this, and it is something I hope to do.

What we would need to do for each of these topics is to re-organize online what they contain *not* in a sequential format like today, but rather in a new, to-be-developed, "fractal" format. This would begin with the single most important thing for students to know and remember as they do their projects, i.e., the one sentence or phrase to remember about that topic for the rest of their lives. For example, for "Project Planning" that top-level sentence might be, "Visualize all the steps in your mind;" for "Negotiation" it might be, "Learn as much as you can about your opponent." In today's education, we do an extremely poor job of focusing kids on the *essence* of what we want them to know about anything. So unlike today's curricula where we begin with the details and leave the key principles to be figured out by the students— or not—in this curriculum we would expect each student to know, by the end of their schooling, the key actionable element(s) of each of the 50 or so topics in the list above. These might be called, in contemporary terms, the "top tweets" (as in Twitter) about each topic. I suggest that, as an exercise, you go back to the list in Figure 9.1 and see if you can state, in just one sentence, the key actionable thing to know about each of the topics. If every kid left K–12 truly knowing the "top tweet" about every one of these topics—and had already applied it to multiple projects—that alone would be a huge step forward in their education.

JUST THE BEGINNING

But that would be just the beginning of the curricular reform we need. We then need to figure out how to expand each topic, both by level of complexity and by ways the topic might apply to various categories and kinds of projects. There might be multiple hierarchies for each topic—one aimed specifically at primary-aged kids, and one at secondary (although experience is far more important than age here). We will need to create a way for a student, through a series of questions, to quickly get to the precise nugget of information he or she needs about any topic as it relates to their project.

NOT "CLASSES" AND "LESSONS"

This expanded, skills-based curriculum would not be acquired by students through classes, lessons, or courses. Rather, as an explicit part of every project, each of the topics, would be considered, *in the project's context*, to see how that particular skill would help. If a teacher, coach, or "empowerer" suggests a student learn more about a particular topic—or if the team members figure this out themselves—any of the topics could be accessed on demand, with the content organized in these new and better ways designed specifically to be of immediate help to students during their projects.

Certain times—perhaps specific days—could be devoted to applying each of the topics to the projects on which students are working—with students reflecting on questions such as, "How does each of the elements of thinking, action, and relationships, apply to my project?" and "How could my project take advantage of a deeper understanding of each of these elements?" Monday, for example, could be the day for them to consider explicitly how to apply Effective Thinking skills to their project, Wednesday might be the day for applying Effective Action skills, and Friday the day for Effective Relationships skills. Each school and class can have broad latitude here in developing effective schemes, and all such schemes should be widely shared and available to anyone.

FOCUSING OUR STUDENTS ON WHAT'S IMPORTANT

One huge, immediate advantage of redefining our core subjects in this new, alternative way is that, unlike the subjects of today, the names of those top-level subjects—Effective Thinking, Effective Action, Effective Relationships, and Effective Accomplishment—make it very clear to the students what their education is really about, what they should become better at, and on what criteria they will be evaluated in life. Few of us care, I submit, if our kids become good at "social studies" as now taught in our schools—but all of us care deeply whether our kids become good at relating and accomplishing. If our kids become good at *all four* of these alternative areas, *and* accomplish 50–100 real-world projects over the course of their K–12 years—*and* leave their school years not with grades but with a résumé of real-world accomplishments—how much better off will they, and we, be?

WHAT ABOUT READING, LITERACY, AND NUMERACY?

No one—certainly not me—wants our kids or our adults to be illiterate or innumerate—on the contrary. But those who see the literacy and numeracy needs of kids in the future only as the same kinds of basic reading and math skills that kids have needed in the past are, I believe, displaying a pre-Internet, "digital immigrant" bias.

Do all kids need to learn basic reading—that is, to decode words on a page? For now, they do—learning to read in the early years is still a huge advantage. But today we can be much better and faster at making this happen. Teaching reading in classes, as we do today, setting aside specific times in the early grades to focus specifically on basic reading skills, may actually be doing our kids a disservice, because reading is a highly individualized task—kids typically learn to read when they have something they want to read. Projects the kids want to do will provide far more incentive to read, and our objective should be to place each kid into project situations where they need reading skills *to achieve something they really want to do*. In such cases, kids will teach themselves—often with the help of their peers—in the same way they teach themselves to play videogames or use any tool. Our role will only be to give them guidance and boosts along the way.

Technologies such as games, apps and the various components of *Sesame Street* are already helping beginning readers understand the necessary underlying principle that words are made up of sounds and that particular letters are associated with those sounds (known, in academia, as "phonemic distinction"). It will be useful to have additional programs that can automatically simplify any text—even abstruse scientific texts—on the fly so that they are available to kids who want that information. There really ought to be an "X-prize" offered to the team that first creates an app not to teach kids to read, but rather to motivate almost any kid to *teach him or herself to read*.

Looking further into the future, and recognizing that the kids we start educating today will not become adults for another one or two decades, we must also realize and acknowledge is that the need for what we call "reading" today—i.e., deciphering the meaning of words on a page (or a screen)— is diminishing, in a very similar way that handwriting already has. The basic technologies that have made this shift possible—text-to-voice and voice-to-text—are improving extremely rapidly, and quickly becoming cheaper and more widespread. In less than a decade, every phone—assuming we still have them and not something better—will likely be able to read out loud whatever is on the screen, at any speed and translated into any language you choose, as well as to write, on the screen or elsewhere, anything you say. It is often forgotten that every single person we view today as "illiterate" can in fact talk—often quite eloquently. It is already becoming less and less necessary to force these people—children or adults—through humiliating reading programs, because there are other alternatives. It will be even less necessary in the future.

It is, of course, the case that writing and reading have been humans' fundamental information storage and retrieval technologies for some time. But despite the amount of writing currently in the world (including on the Internet) we need to begin leading our kids in new directions. Remember, our kids will spend most of their lives living decades from now, a time when need for today's kind of reading are likely to be vastly different. Many educators already realize that the meaning of "literacy" is expanding rapidly in our times to include many types of visual literacy, such as video as well as "programming" and "coding." And even those last skills might become obsolete in our kids' lifetimes, as their computers get better at learning from experience.[25]

Regarding numeracy, now that machines to which more and more kids have almost universal access (i.e. that are in their pockets) can do basic computation and calculation, those formerly-essential skills are no longer what we need to be spending a great deal of time teaching our kids. Instead, we need to get much better at teaching them to see the math in real-world situations, and to understand the kind and magnitude of answers to expect. People often cite as negative, for example, the fact that many of our kids cannot "make change" at a store. But that is a job, more and more frequently, for machines. What humans still need is to have a rough idea of how much change there should be—for example, $5, $10, $20, or $50—calculating the precise amount has now become the machine's role. If our machines break down, or the power goes out, we find a temporary solution, fix the problem, and move on, just as we do when our cars break down; we don't spend years teaching all our kids to master horseback riding as a backup.

What our kids really need to know about math is how to find a good enough approximation, along with an order of magnitude—a skill that is often *lost* in today's process of algorithmic calculation by hand. Prior to the computer era, our engineers—among our most numerate people—used slide rules that showed only a three-digit approximation of the answer, to which they had to add the decimal point (i.e. the order of magnitude). The engineers knew that's the real math skill humans still need.

AND WHAT ABOUT ALL OUR CURRENT "MESS" CONTENT?

People often ask, "If we change to a Better Their World education, what will happen to today's huge amount of subject area "content"? Is it all needed? Will it all just "go away"? Will our kids become, as one person put it to me, "barbarians?"

The need for *some* math, language arts, science, and social studies content and skills—different for every student—will of course never completely disappear, and all the various aspects of these subjects will, in the future, always be available to students and anyone who needs them. But they will not be, as they are today, "core material" to be learned, in detail and in advance of any need, by everyone. Math, language arts, science, and social studies are important in different ways, and to differing degrees, to each individual—based on that person's strengths, interests, and passions. *They are not needed, or useful, in the same way for everybody.* As students accomplish their projects, each of them will find out, with their teachers' help, what MESS components they need and how to get them. They can be guided, as individuals or teams, as the need arises, to find this information.

The amount of "content" that *everyone* truly needs is surprisingly small and high-level. It probably includes little more than a high-level knowledge of the layout of the world and of its diversity, the major arcs of human history, the major tenets of science, and some knowledge of how we govern ourselves. All the rest is detail, useful only to some.

On the other hand, Effective Thinking, Effective Action, Effective Relationships, and Effective Accomplishment are important to *all* students at *every* grade level. It is crucial for an effective education that every student focus on becoming as good as they possibly can at each of these overarching skills.

What's more, I believe that everyone, at some level, knows this. Parents know it. Educators know it. And most importantly, kids know it.

THE NEW MATRIX

Here is what the new "schematic matrix" for a Better Their World education looks like (Figure 9.2).

Figure 9.2.

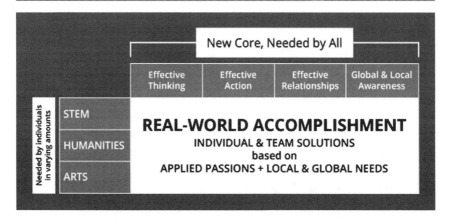

The projects are the central focus of the education, and the curriculum supports the accomplishment of those projects. The core subjects that all students need—Effective Thinking, Action, and Relationships (along with Global and Local Awareness)—are across the top, and the STEM (science, technology, engineering and mathematics), humanities, and arts that each student needs in different measures are down the side.

In the Better Their World education the "side" components will be almost completely individualized. Let's now take a closer look at the "top" components, that is, the "new core" that is needed by all, i.e. Effective Thinking, Effective Action and Effective Relationships and Global and Local Awareness.

EFFECTIVE THINKING

Academic education has always focused on on particular kinds of thinking such as quantitative thinking (mathematics) and thinking about texts (basic and "deep" reading). Today, in many places there is an increased emphasis on critical thinking and problem solving. But effective thinking is actually far broader than what most academic education provides. Here are some of the components that would be in the Effective Thinking portion of the Education to Better Their World curriculum:

Quantitative and Pattern
  Thinking
Understanding
  Communication
Critical Thinking
Problem Solving (Individual
  and Collective)
Scientific Thinking
Situational Awareness
Historical Perspective
Creative Thinking
Design Thinking
Integrative Thinking
Systems Thinking
Financial Thinking

Inquiry
Argument
Judgment
Transfer
Aesthetics
Habits of Mind
Growth Mindset
Focus
Stress Control
Concentration
Contemplation and
  Meditation
Self-Knowledge of One's
  Passions, Strengths, and
  Weaknesses

Almost anyone would, I believe, agree that all of these components are important. Yet today, other than the first three or four, these are *not* skills that all kids are taught, or that all kids acquire, in today's K–12 academic curriculum.

Of course, *some* teachers and *some* schools include *some* of them. But they are not offered to our kids *systematically* in ways that are likely to get them acquired. The only skills we do teach *systematically to all* are reading and quantitative thinking (note that those are the only two components of the SAT test). More recently, scientific thinking, critical thinking, and problem solving are more frequently included in this group. But a great many other "thinking" skills, including the extremely important skills of design thinking, systems thinking, judgment, aesthetics, habits of mind, and self-knowledge of one's own passions and strengths (and of course others), are *not* presented to kids in any systematic way as part of our curriculum. And even those areas that *are* taught are often approached more in terms of "content" than of "thinking."

One sad result of this approach is that today, many adults who deal with the people who emerge from our K–12 schools believe that—despite all these years of education—our young people haven't "learned to think." I hear college teachers frequently comment that "I have to teach my students to think." I hear business executives complain about their employees' inability to solve problems. College or the workplace is far too late to be starting this—our kids should have been spending a much larger portion of their K–12 time acquiring effective thinking skills. Effective Thinking—presented in ways that are far more effective than we do it today—should certainly be a top-level subject for every student.

Many academics argue that thinking has to be "domain-grounded" (i.e. done in a specific context), and while there are differences of opinion on the subject, those people may very well be right. But *which* domain doesn't matter, as long as kids learn to do their thinking well. All of the fundamentals of good thinking can be learned by considering situations and problems in whatever area is of interest to each individual student. We need to help all our student think effectively *in the context of accomplishing*.

There are some things, of course, that we would like *all* of our kids to think about—ethics and forms of government, for example. But there are, I believe, many fewer of these than most think. A key principle in education should be, "General skills for all, individual examples for each student."

What we really must do is help each kid find his or her own real-world problems to analyze. We do not need a textbook full of "officially appropriate" or "relevant" problems, because *any* problem of appropriate scope and level can be used to teach the components of effective thinking. We will never run out of these.

The positive result of doing this is that we will focus our students' attention far less on the subject matter, and far more on the ways they approach thinking about it. After applying Effective Thinking to projects for 13 years, students will come out of school able to think effectively about *almost any* problem or issue, in multiple ways—wearing multiple "thinking caps", as Edward de Bono puts it in his book *Six Thinking Hats* (de Bono, 1985) [26]. Our young people will also be able to recognize which types of thinking are *ineffective* in particular situations—something that today's kids are not, for the most part, focused on or good at.

GLOBAL AND LOCAL AWARENESS

There is a particular component of Effective Thinking that deserves to be considered separately. I believe we want all of kids to be globally and locally "situationally aware" (a term frequently used by the military, and in driver education and personal safety/defense classes) about their world. Our kids need to be continually looking around and considering the issues and problems that are critical to them, the means and projects they will choose to address those problems, and whether those means and projects will, indeed, "better their world." As students do projects, both in school and in life, it is crucial that they continually check back on whether they are truly addressing the issues that matter to their world and to them.

BUT THINKING, ALONE, IS NOT ENOUGH

So we certainly can—and I believe we must—teach Effective Thinking more specifically, more systematically, and better than we do today in our curriculum, and do it "just in time" as kids accomplish their projects. But, unfortunately, a huge part of our educational problem today is that most school curricula are *only* about thinking. Other huge domains that are crucial for life and success—particularly acting, relating, and accomplishing—are almost entirely missing. This is the legacy of our academic tradition alone having gone into our schools. The new Better Their World curriculum is a deliberate attempt to address and repair this unhelpful situation.

EFFECTIVE ACTION

Many of us are familiar with people who know lots of things but can't do much. One good explanation for this is that we don't teach—or hardly ever teach—effective action in school. But we certainly could.

Thanks to Stephen R. Covey, for example, the "Seven habits of highly effective people" ™ have been known and recognized for over a quarter of a century (Covey, 1989)[27]. What justification can there possibly be for our being aware of these incredibly important habits, yet not teaching them to our kids? Our kids should be practicing these habits every day and with every project. (Covey's seven habits are: "Be proactive;" "Begin with the end in mind;" "Put first things first;" "Think win–win;" "Seek first to understand, then to be understood;" "Synergize;" and "Sharpen the saw.") Ironically, his company, FranklinCovey, has even developed a curriculum to teach these habits to students, so we already have good ideas about how to do it. Yet while some schools use this curriculum, most do not.

Components of Effective Action that we could and should be transmitting to our kids (in addition to writing and research, which are pretty much the only actions we currently do) are:

The Habits of Highly Effective People	Resilience and "Grit"
	Entrepreneurship
Body Awareness and Health Management	Innovation
	Improvisation
Agility	Ingenuity
Adaptability	Strategy and Tactics
Leadership and Followership	Stewardship
Decision Making Under Uncertainty	Breaking Barriers
	Project Management
Experimentation	Programming Machines
Prudent Risk-Taking	Making Effective Videos
Reality Testing/Feedback	Innovating with Current and Future Technologies
Patience	

We may tell our kids we want them to be resilient, for example, but we don't typically *show them how* to apply resilience to projects they do over their entire K–12 years—even though it's a skill acquired largely through practice over time.

In almost all of these "Effective Action" areas there are experts, often with already developed curricular materials. Angela Duckworth, for example, specializes in "grit" (Duckworth, 2016)[28] Project management is a well-established and highly useful discipline, valuable in any walk of life, yet it is rarely taught or learned in K–12. There exist, around the world, curricula for teaching entrepreneurship and creativity, but few of our K–12 schools use them. Why are all these curricula unavailable to our students in a form that they can not only understand, but immediately use and apply to their projects? All that is needed is to reformulate the existing material in ways that would be memorable and immediately useful to kids doing projects. We *could* do this, and doing so would be incredibly helpful to our kids. Imagine what our kids could accomplish if we gave them these resources.

EFFECTIVE RELATIONSHIPS

Many consider building and maintaining effective relationships to be the most important skill a person can possess. Relationships, of course, often come up in school—in classrooms, in projects, and in literature. Yet how much of our curriculum is devoted to systematically analyzing those relationships, with the goal of applying them to accomplish their projects *and* making students better at building and maintaining their own effective relationships—despite the fact that the study of relationships is deep and well known. Curricula on emotional intelligence and social skills already exist, but—despite some recent efforts in this direction[29]—they are not widely used or applied.

Many teachers *do* try to help kids deal with one-on-one relationships and issues as they occur in the classroom (although not, as a rule, as part of the curriculum). But they could also be helping their students to become far more effective at building and maintaining relationships in teams, families, communities, workplaces, and, of course, online, particularly if materials were available.

We could also, in the context of the projects, systematically help our kids to become more effective at skills that help build effective relationships, such as empathy, ethics, politics, citizenship, negotiation, and conflict resolution. Again, for almost all of these there already exist curricula created by various interested academics and groups, such as the Karras program in negotiation that is highly advertised in airline magazines. Yet, even schools that claim their objective is a "more peaceful world" do not always offer their students core knowledge about conflict resolution—although such curricula do exist.

Here are some of the components of effective relationships:

Communication and
  Collaboration:
- One-on-one
- In teams
- In families
- In communities
- At work
- Online
- In virtual worlds
- With machines

Listening
Networking
Relationship building
Empathy

Courage
Compassion
Tolerance
Ethics
Politics
Citizenship
Conflict Resolution
Negotiation
Coaching and
  Being Coached
Peer-to-Peer
Mentoring and
  Being Mentored

What if we made building and maintaining effective relationships a key pillar of the world's curriculum, and something that we want all our kids to acquire?

EFFECTIVE ACCOMPLISHMENT

Of all the things missing from today's curriculum, not teaching our kids systematically about *accomplishment in the real world* is perhaps our greatest failing. If we did, it could improve so many important things in their, and our, world. Today, we essentially waste almost all the enormous potential "accomplishing power" of our youth by not requiring them to use it and showing them how to do so effectively.

Imagine, for example, if "first grade" in any of the world's poor villages lacking a water cistern was about building such a cistern, and "second grade" was about building a water purification system, and "third grade" about building a Wi-Fi system, and so on. The same principle, of course, could apply to any place, rich or poor—just substitute whatever they are missing and need, e.g. facilities for seniors, better connectivity, etc. Each year, old solutions would be improved, new problems would be addressed, and more would get done.

We stopped our kids from working in the real world in former times because the kids were often physically exploited. But times are now different. Much of what needs to be done in the world today no longer requires physical work, but rather intellectual work (e.g., designing, creating, and coding on computers). So "Child Labor 2.0," if you will, can be both benign and useful to all.

All kids, even our youngest, love to work on real, important projects. Many get joy just from knowing they are useful. Most can figure out how to manage themselves, both as individuals and groups, particularly as they get older and particularly with our guidance when needed. Students of all ages, joined together in increasingly powerful networks, ought to be accomplishing enormous numbers of desperately needed things in the world—not just in their local areas, but in nations and businesses around the globe.

All of these projects and accomplishments would give our kids powerful and valuable experience—not just for education, but for life. Our education would produce kids distinguished not by their grade point average, but by what they have accomplished in the world. We should not only be encouraging this, but we should be re-structuring our education to help kids do it systematically, throughout their K–12 years.

MORE WORK TO DO

Obviously, the development of a new curriculum around these ideas and themes, especially one designed not to be taught academically but rather to be acquired as needed for projects, requires considerable work that has not yet been done. I will be encouraging, supporting, and documenting this work at the Global Future Education Foundation (www.global-future-education.org). I invite everyone to join me in the process.

CHAPTER 10

Supporting New Education with Technology

Today's educational technology is almost all geared to supporting our
old, academic paradigm;
what we need is educational technology for the new paradigm of
Bettering Their World.

TODAY, TECHNOLOGY STILL STRUGGLES to find its place in an academic educational context that was born, and long survived, without
it. Is our modern technology more useful to an Education to Better
Their World?

BETTERING THE WORLD DOES NOT *REQUIRE* TECHNOLOGY . . .

An Education to Better Their World does not *require* any technology—it
is not just a technology-enabled form of education. Rather, it's an education whose ends are to empower all kids to be able to take action to
improve their own world and to see themselves as having agency. No
modern technology is necessary for project teams to accomplish many
things that are world-improving—from bettering relationships between
groups in their communities, to fixing up neighborhoods, to restoring
historic artifacts. A Better Their World education is therefore not just
useful to or good for only those kids in the world fortunate enough
have access to all the latest devices and services. Such an education
can be undertaken anywhere—from the most isolated places to the
poorest pockets of society—and will benefit that place's kids and community. All that is required is that educators and parents see the ends
of education not as just improving individuals in an academic sense but
as bettering their world—and that they see their job as empowering
kids further to do so.

. . . BUT THE MORE KIDS HAVE ACCESS TO TECHNOLOGY, THE MORE THEY CAN BETTER THEIR WORLD

With that understood, we can also say that having access to technology can certainly help kids to Better Their World in major ways. Modern technology is becoming a part of more and more kids' lives in more and more places. As it does, that technology will continue to empower those kids to do more—technology will almost certainly be a big part of almost everything most kids accomplish in the future.

Though not required for everything, technology *is* a big empowering factor. So we need to consider what technology's role can and should be in a Better Their World education. How can new technologies, to the extent kids have access to them, be used in the most fruitful way to support the projects of Better Their World education and to educate the empowered kids of today and tomorrow?

I believe we also need to ask another important question: Is creating dedicated educational technology helping our move to a new educational vision, or is it, in fact, holding us back?

TECHNOLOGY AS A MASK

How, you might ask, could educational technology possibly be holding back our kids and our education? The answer is twofold. First, technology often slows down our traditional academic education as our current teachers struggle to use it. But far more importantly, most of the technology used in schools today is about nothing more than doing "old things in new ways." We use technology only to do things we could do before—like deliver content, or do research, or keep records—in faster and sometimes marginally better ways. We convince ourselves that by introducing these technologies into our schools and by using the technologies in these ways, we are doing something to move our kids' education forward and prepare them for the future. But, educationally, we are not doing anything new or different at all. Introducing technology—something we often do with great fanfare and expense—very often masks our lack of any real educational progress. This—and not just the fact that some technology may be uncomfortable for teachers to use—may be a key reason that technology meets so much resistance from many of our experienced teachers.

VAULTING THE "EDUCATION CUSP"

A metaphor I often find helpful in understanding the current state of the world's education is that of an "education cusp" (see Figure 10.1). On the left side of the cusp is the academic and achievement-based education of today, and on the right is the world-improving, accomplishment-based education of tomorrow. As the diagram shows, there is a very high and sharp cusp or barrier between the two models of education. To get to an Education to Better Their World we have to, in some sense, "vault" over this cusp. The principal element that is needed to vault the cusp is a change in how we view the ends of education.

But what is the role of technology in vaulting the cusp to an Education to Better Their World? Does technology have a different role to play in Bettering Their World than it does in an academic education?

THE COMING OF "ED TECH"

Although it took what many felt was too long to arrive, educational technology, or "ed tech," has finally entered the mainstream in many places. Schools around the world are acquiring and having their students use more and more technology. The business of creating technology designed specifically for education is now rapidly growing—some might say exploding—with new products appearing almost daily. Funders,

Figure 10.1.

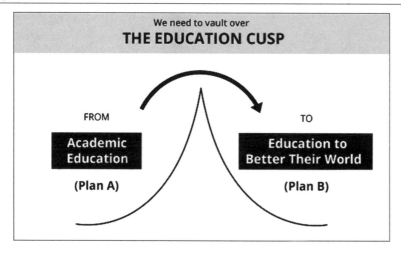

incubators, and venture capital firms in California's Silicon Valley and elsewhere are eagerly searching for education companies and technologies to invest in. Money for ed tech startups is flowing—in the United States alone, ed tech ventures raised close to $2 billion in 2015.[30] Is all this investment helping us or hindering us in our quest to vault the cusp to an Education to Better Their World?

GENERAL, OR DEDICATED?

In a general sense, almost all new technologies empower those kids who have access to them—technology allows them to control more and more of their world. The more that new, advanced technologies spread around the globe—the more features that personal devices have, the greater the number of kids who have the devices in their pockets (or soon, perhaps, embedded under their skin), and the more kids have access to fast and powerful networks and Internet connections—the more powerful our kids become to act and accomplish. There is no doubt that the spread of general, non-education-specific technologies—including phones, apps, social connections, and collaboration and sharing tools, all powerfully networked together—will empower all our young people further. Getting these technologies into the hands of all kids should certainly be a huge priority for the world and for all who are interested in education.

USING GENERALLY AVAILABLE TECHNOLOGY POWERFULLY

Of course, just having these tools and technologies is not enough—kids have to use them powerfully to solve problems. Kids are just beginning to figure out how to use available technologies for accomplishing important things, and not just for recreation. An early example is the setting up of impromptu events and "pop-ups" by students. One great advantage of the coming real, world-improving, accomplishment-based education is that our kids will have to figure out—by themselves and in teams—how to use their personal, general-purpose technologies in the most powerful ways to get real and meaningful work and projects done. They will need to decide how to use technologies such as real-time video communication, simulation tools, robotics, and artificial intelligence to accomplish projects that Better Their World.

ED TECH IS ONLY FOR "ACADEMIC" EDUCATION

Academic education has struggled mightily with these "general" technologies—from spreadsheets, to calculators, to search, to artificial intelligence. It has struggled with whether and how to add them, how to integrate them, and how to teach kids to use them "properly." Their success at integrating non-education-specific technologies has been, at best, mixed.

So a new category of technology has emerged in the world—"ed tech" i.e. "dedicated" educational technology, whose only use is for education and educational settings. And since academic education is currently pretty much the only education we have, just about all of this dedicated educational technology is—not surprisingly—designed to support that education. Pretty much all the ed tech products created around the world today are designed to support academic education in some way.

Today, in addition to the general purpose, widely available tools that almost all kids have (or will have) access to, we also have these specialized, dedicated products. Some of them, like Khan Academy, are free and trying hard to stay that way. Others, however, cost real money. How valuable to our kids' future are the kinds of specific "educational technology" tools that we currently fund, create, and provide for education? How much are they helping educate our kids for that future? How much effort and money should we continue to put into designing them? How valuable might they be for an Education to Better Their World? The answers to all those are questions are, I believe, still open.

THE UNDERLYING PREMISE

The underlying premise of the ed tech industry is that dedicated tools do, indeed, help academic education. The big bet of the entire sector is that they can convince enough people that they do to buy them in order to justify the massive investment.

I believe many of today's ed tech tools can help do—or can even take over—many of the tasks of academic education. These tasks include providing kids with content, managing that content, helping enhance kids' knowledge and thinking skills in certain areas, evaluating kids' progress, preventing "cheating," and many others. The ed tech firms have by now produced tens of thousands and maybe even hundreds of thousands of products to do these things: academic-education-supporting technology products range from new ways to present and deliver content (e.g., through video); to new ways to record, store, and analyze and apply student information (e.g., through "big data" analyses); to new ways to supposedly make teaching and measurement easier (e.g., through programs that answer questions and do computer-based testing).

Yet people are still debating to what extent all these products have helped make our academic education "better." The data are, at best, mixed, and proponents on both sides are still making their arguments. Many education reformers not involved with technology remain skeptical. "The people in Silicon Valley think technology will solve everything," says one observer. "It won't. There's a human side to education that won't go away." Others do not see the improvements they had expected from technology. Still others think that technology has not been used in the right ways. To what extent these products will replace, rather than enhance, the work of our human teachers remains a hotly contested topic.

WHERE TO ADD VALUE?

But one thing, I believe, *is* clear: Almost all the ed tech start-ups today represent attempts to add value only to the left side of the cusp by making our current academic education more engaging, more efficient, more effective, better at data collection and feedback, and/or easier for teachers to provide. These start-ups are not attempting to move us over the cusp to something new. This is, no doubt, because the profitability of the ed tech market is still very much dependent on academic educational institutions.

Some helpful products have and will continue to come out of such efforts. But too many of those products may—unhelpfully for kids—wind up helping our academic education to survive long beyond the time its usefulness has expired. An example is test preparation apps, which, by doing a better job of preparing kids for high-stakes tests, make it less likely that those tests will go away.

SHORT TERM VS. LONG-TERM

Although technologies supporting academic K–12 education may make economic sense in the near-term, they make little sense for where education needs to be headed in the longer term. From a long-term perspective, the approach of creating new and expensive technology just to do the same old education in different ways is, perhaps, the most wasteful use of our resources for educating our kids there is. Using technology in this way both trivializes technology's real potential and fails to empower our kids further to do anything new that they need. Compared to how technology *could* be helping our kids become educated for the future, using ed tech only—or mainly—to do "old things better" is trivial—no matter what the complexity and sophistication level of the products themselves.

Already, today, there's a losing battle going on the left side of the cusp: As more and more products are funded and emerge, many academic K–12 teachers are becoming reluctant to keep trying new product after new product only to marginally improve what they already have and do. So it is becoming harder for any new academic product or "innovation" to get a lasting foothold in schools. Even big players with deep pockets and strong academic educational credentials stumble here, as did media mogul Rupert Murdoch and former Chancellor of the New York City school system Joel Klein with Amplify, News Corp's well-funded and highly touted startup to create new educational tablets. (After a big initial investment, it failed ignominiously.)

POWERFUL, NOT TRIVIAL

The ed tech that most companies offer today will not get us over the cusp to the education kids really need. Our kids require technologies that not only empower them further to do new things (e.g., connect around the globe, collaborate in new ways, simulate), but that also, in doing so, support real-world accomplishment in powerful ways.

Far too many of today's ed tech products—technically advanced and sophisticated though they may be—serve to keep our education rooted firmly on the old side of the cusp by providing us with new means to continue to do the things we could already do before technology arrived. For those who believe academic education will continue to be successful and thrive in the future, this may be fine. But if you believe that education is evolving to a new paradigm, then ed tech is masking what is going on—making it look as if we are making progress while actually preventing us from moving forward.

In some cases, technology may make academic education marginally more engaging for kids, or marginally "better" or easier for educators to deliver. But delivering the old education better should be neither our goal nor the goal of our educational technology, because the world has changed, and a new education is required. Today's ed tech may serve to prop up academic education for a time (although there is still much resistance). But metaphorically, it is doing nothing but "rearranging the deck chairs on the Titanic."

The success rate of ed tech startups is, today, very low.[31] I suspect this is, in large measure, because ed tech companies are trying to compete and "out-innovate" one another within the narrow parameters set by the old, academic education. Propping up a failing system is a losing long-term strategy.

ALREADY MOOT?

Although the creation of academic ed tech products (and the discussions about their effectiveness) will go on for some time—with people continuing to jump into the industry and create new "solutions" and companies—the answer to whether technology truly makes academic K–12 education better may already be moot because K–12 education itself, as we have seen throughout this book, is morphing into something new and better—an Education to Better Their World. And the ed tech industry's almost exclusive focus on academic education is actually holding that progress back. As the world's educational model evolves from academic education to empowering kids to Better Their World, and as the means of education evolves from just "learning" to real, world-improving accomplishment, our concept of the role of technology in education, and of what ed-tech can and should do for us, needs to evolve as well.

A DIFFERENT APPROACH TO EDUCATIONAL TECHNOLOGY

I believe there are many technology creators who already envision the kind of real, world-improving, accomplishment-based education that I have described in this book (and that is on the right-hand side of the education cusp)—who not only agree it is coming but want to help make it happen. But those people have not as yet vaulted the cusp in terms of the technology they create. Many companies and educators who see the need to move to something new for our kids find themselves "impaled" on the education cusp's sharp inflection point between two worlds: Because it is not yet clear what kinds of dedicated educational products (if any) will support the Better Their

World paradigm, innovators have to experiment. But the small, barely emerging Better Their World market (if there is one) doesn't support the kinds of infrastructure, overhead, and business models companies have built for the large, worldwide academic K–12 market.

"Impaled on the cusp" is a highly uncomfortable place to be. Unfortunately, as the world moves to a new education paradigm, the failure rate of ed tech companies may reach close to 100% before the real solutions we need are created. It is, in a sense, the classic "innovator's dilemma," whereby most are innovating only on the margins, and some new groups will, as the paradigm changes, disrupt their way out of the old education and into the mainstream with new and better products that serve the directions in which education is moving.[32]

So it is now time, I believe, to stop focusing almost all ed tech innovation and start-up money on ways of marginally improving the outdated and expiring academic educational system and to begin creating products for education's—and our kids'—future. Although some of the marginally better products that emerge will no doubt provide some return on investment—and even help prop up the old academic K–12 paradigm for a while—academic education will be disrupted and superseded, despite its current ubiquity, because it no longer fits the needs of our kids and our world.

ED TECH FOR BETTERING THEIR WORLD

Technology—both general and dedicated—will, I strongly believe, play a big role in supporting a Better their World education model, and we should be doing our best to create new technologies that help us get over the cusp to an Education to Better Their World. Up until now, few technologies and products have been created that directly support real, world-improving, project-based education. It is time for our technology entrepreneurs and companies to begin designing, creating, and promoting such Better Their World technology products that will help educators and students vault the cusp more quickly and get to Education to Better Their World more easily. The best role for educational technology start-ups and researchers today is to begin thinking about and building products for replacing the academic K–12 education system we have today and moving toward supporting an Education that Betters Their World. Since we already have a good idea of what that education that will look like, we should start work now on supporting it.

NEW KINDS OF PRODUCTS

What kinds of dedicated products would support real-world, accomplishment-based education? What might these products look like? One early example of a technology product that does this is dosomething.org—a helpful out-of-school application enabling kids to match up with projects on a self-selected basis.

Other useful products would include the following:

- databases for projects (both done and proposed)
- databases of potential volunteer project advisors in a wide variety of different areas
- technologies for team-based collaboration, for tracking projects' progress, and for getting help when needed
- technologies for companies, NGOs, and governments to propose, assign, track, and evaluate projects
- technologies for teams to get input and feedback on projects
- technologies for creating post-mortems on project teams' experiences
- technologies to curate videos of kids talking about their projects, discussing the problems they experienced and how they overcame them
- coaching tips from and for teachers and project leaders
- elements of the supporting curriculum

We don't yet know what most of these products will look like—we hope our entrepreneurs and developers, like our kids, will surprise us.

KEY QUESTIONS FOR FUNDERS AND DEVELOPERS

The key questions ed tech funders and entrepreneurs should be asking are these: How do we support—with dedicated technology—an education that has all our kids adding value to the world by doing real-world projects, accomplishing important things, and solving real problems in areas where we really need the help that kids can provide? Are there better tools for teamwork and collaboration? For evaluating and disseminating projects and results? Are there young-person-friendly versions of tools already used in business? (Or can our kids—being in many cases more technologically sophisticated than adults—begin doing as students advanced things that our adults currently don't yet do?)

Are there specific tools we can create that will help kids do projects in particular areas, such as infrastructure improvement, historical preservation, science, healthcare, government, and environmental protection? How do we support with technology an education whose goal is not just learning but helping all our students become good, effective, and world-improving people? How do we support with technology an education that is based on a far broader set of skills than today's MESS, (a skill set that includes, in addition to a broader definition of "thinking," the almost universally excluded domains of "relationships" (including social and emotional), "action," and "real-world accomplishment")? How do we support with technology an education that is focused on a keen awareness of improving the local and global world in which our kids live and on identifying, amplifying, and developing kids' individual passions in and for that world—rather than on having them master a set of (often outdated) subjects?

The answers to these questions are the support our kids really need from educational technology.

TECNOLOGY AS A NEW FOUNDATION

It is likely that technology (both dedicated and general) will be as foundational for our new Better Their World education as reading and writing have been for the old, academic one. We just don't yet know how to create the technology to support Better Their World education, so we are still in the early stages of experimentation. There are no doubt fundamental new educational infrastructures we should be building, such as databases of projects, systems for matching students to projects, and new ways of presenting a much broader and supportive curriculum. We also need technology's help in transforming our current content-providing teachers into the coaches and empowerers we need, as we will discuss in the next chapter. What other supports should we be building in addition to these?

As these new Education to Better Their World–supporting technologies are created, we can test them within the worldwide PBL movement and in the many schools, colleges, and universities that currently offer service, capstone, and other projects. Those places may not only provide good feedback, but they can also help create developers who design additional products we need.

Ed tech entrepreneurs should also be looking to learn more from the companies—Facebook, Google, YouTube, Amazon, Apple, and others—that are already, in fact, conducting the world's largest educational experiments. YouTube may have already become the world's single largest educator—people of all ages now go there first to learn—for free, from both peers and experts—about almost everything. These companies should be doing more to make their sharing, social cooperation, and collaboration tools more useful—not just to academic educators but to kids doing real, world-improving projects. Given that these same companies are also at the forefront of businesses calling for employees who can do and accomplish far more than our academic graduates can today, the companies should be looking for and creating educational products to help real-world projects get done in educational setttings—based, possibly, on technologies they have already created internally for their employees. A useful thing to note is how unafraid these companies are to experiment as they see the world, and their customers, quickly evolve.

BOTTOM LINE

For educational technology to truly help education and our kids move forward, it should be moving away from supporting the old academic educational paradigm and toward helping to create the new and emerging the real, world-improving, accomplishment-based Education to Better Their World. Today we see the first sprouts of Better Their World–supporting technology emerging (e.g., at dosomething.org). Those sprouts desperately need funding, support, and cultivation. And we need many more of them.

Ask yourself: How can technology help kids identify, explore, and grow through applying their passion? How can technology connect kids efficiently to the kinds of real-world projects that will be their education in the future? How can technology support kids' becoming good, effective, and world-improving people? How can technology help teachers shift to a new way of thinking about what education means in our new world?

These are certainly the questions that all ed tech start-ups should be asking—and some are. Those ed tech start-ups and companies that move in these directions—i.e., over the cusp and into the new and future educational landscape—are the ones that will truly add long-term value to our kids and the ones that will survive and thrive in our new and emerging technology-filled world. Marginally improving our outdated academic system with ed tech is of very little long-term value to our kids, our economy, and our society. We need to use our powerful new technologies to help vault the cusp to the new Education to Better Their World paradigm.

CHAPTER 11

The Changing Role of the Teacher in Educating Our Kids
From Content Provider to Empowerer

"It took me only a summer to change."

—Jenny Henry, fifth grade teacher in Douglas County, CO

AND WHAT OF OUR TEACHERS? Adult guidance is key, I believe, for young people to become prepared for and to thrive in their future. While there are many adults who influence our kids—from parents, to family, to role models—we have passed a great deal of the responsibility for preparing our kids for their future to our teachers. Today, there are somewhere between 10 and 20 million primary and secondary teachers in the world—including approximately two million in the United States. Our kids spend a huge amount of their formative time with them. They are crucial for our kids' development. At their best, they offer kids things no machine can provide, including empathy, respect, passion, and motivation. Even with all our new and quickly advancing technology, our need for great human teachers is unlikely to go away in the foreseeable future.

But to be helpful, adults must offer kids the *right* guidance. Today, our kids'—and the world's—educational needs are changing in profound ways. To meet those needs, teachers must change and evolve. The key question they—and we all—need to be asking is this:

"What should our teachers be doing, during the time they spend with our kids, to best serve and prepare those kids for their future?"

The answer to this question has already started to change dramatically in our new age and context. My guess is that every single person who works daily in a classroom already senses that huge changes are taking place not just in the world, but in our kids—what they can do, what they want to do, and what they should be doing. Most teachers know that these changes impact how they need to use their time with kids to best effect. Many teachers around the world are already taking, steps, in a variety of ways, to make changes.

I will discuss in the next chapter the likelihood of change ever coming to mainstream education (hint: I am optimistic). In this chapter I want to help as many teachers as possible move forward in new and positive directions by outlining the trajectory that I believe teaching is taking in the world and by providing teachers who want to be on that trajectory with an evolutionary path to the future.

A POSITIVE OPPORTUNITY—AND AN EVOLUTIONARY PATH TOWARD IT

The emerging change in the ends of education from individual accomplishment to bettering their world dramatically impacts how our teachers need to be spending their time. We already see, in many scattered places, changes in the teaching profession that point the way to the future. These changes offer a hugely positive opportunity for all of us—teachers, students, and society.

Almost all of us understand, I believe, that educators have to adapt their behavior to meet our kids'—and our world's—future needs. Doing so will require courage—not just from our teachers, but from all of us. Although not everyone welcomes changes in their established routines and work life, it is enormously important that we not let our fear of change overcome us, or block us from making the kinds of adaptations we need. The very definition of courage is "feeling the fear and doing what is needed anyway."

THE TEACHING PROFESSION IS CHANGING—AS ALL PROFESSIONS ARE

The message of this book is that a new and better kind of K–12 education is emerging in the world, and that the path to get there is becoming clearer. This is true for the path that teachers must traverse as well. It is not a quick path nor an easy path for everyone. It will certainly require some support from above, and it is likely that not all will choose to take it.

But this emerging path is something that every person who wants to hold the position of "teacher" in the future must understand and consider. Some have already started down the road—we will meet two of them shortly. My sense is that in the long run, almost all teachers will eventually choose to take this path, first, because it is the right path to meet our kids' needs, and second, because the psychological rewards for those who take the path are potentially enormous.

As our teachers begin to alter their practice, they will be in the company of almost every other professional in the world. All professions are now going through profound adaptations to our new world and context. Medical professionals are evolving their focus from curing the sick to helping people stay well, as their patients' information and needs change. Airline pilots are evolving their skill sets from physically and mechanically controlling the planes, to solving problems when things go wrong, as our planes begin to fly themselves. I'm sure you can think of other examples.

The teaching profession is evolving as well.

THE TRAJECTORY

The overall trajectory of the change in the teaching profession is from the teacher being "the person who stands at the front of a room delivering prescribed content to classes of kids," to "the teacher being a person who coaches and empowers teams of kids doing real, world-improving projects." Rather than telling students how to do things and then making sure they did them right, the future teacher provides guidance to kids on how to choose projects that will help them acquire needed skills, and then assists them in getting their projects accomplished effectively. It is a shift, in brief, from "content providing and direct instruction" to "coaching and empowering kids." Or as some have said, from "sage on the stage" to "guide on the side," with "guide" being an extremely powerful and important role.

To go from one end of the trajectory to the other requires following an "evolutionary pathway." That pathway is what the remainder of this chapter is about.

THE "EVOLUTIONARY PATHWAY"

Over the centuries, the world has created a universally recognized profession—teaching—with a professional corps of practitioners—teachers—to help prepare our kids for the future. Today, most of these teachers, no matter where in the world they are from, can easily identify with others in their profession. That is because pretty much all of them were educated and trained in the same overall system—the academic educational system that is today ubiquitous in the world and that practically all of us who attended school went through. Although its details vary from place to place, what all of academic education requires from teachers, at its core, is content delivery. Currently, most of the content to be delivered lies in the four areas of math, language, science, and social studies ("The MESS") and delivery is done through direct instruction—although there are, increasingly, other content areas, and other means of delivering content. The "content" itself can range from material to be memorized and learned by rote, to material to which kids must apply complex, higher-order thinking skills—and to those skills themselves.

Today, just about all the world's teachers are academic teachers, and most of us have in our mind—whatever the content being delivered—an ideal of what a great teacher is. He or she "knows the material cold," "explains well and is a great communicator," "provides innovative instruction," "keeps students engaged and under control," "is an inspiration to students," "makes kids achieve better grades and graduate." This paradigm of what a great teacher should be and do is now deeply ingrained in many people's minds.

But it is important to understand that this ideal in the public's mind of what a great teacher is, and does, applies almost entirely to *one particular kind* of education, i.e. academic education. Only academic education is a hierarchy-based system in which the teachers are at the top, in control, and manage (and often micromanage) the students. Only academic education requires continual explanation from teachers to an entire class at once. Only academic education has as its paradigmatic model that the teacher stand at the front of the room and that the students remain seated and well-controlled by the teacher at almost all times. Academic teaching can be done more strictly or less strictly, but the role for the teacher is the same everywhere—delivering content to students.

THE STRUGGLE

Content delivery, however, is no longer the best way, or the right way, to teach kids for the future. Today, every academic teacher faces and is struggling with (or needs to struggle with) a major issue—an issue not of their own making, but one with which they all have to deal nonetheless. The issue is that academic education no longer works as well for today's kids as it did for kids in the past. Today, the academic K–12 paradigm—despite myriad and continuous attempts to improve it—is failing in many cases, and is starting to become obsolete.

As the world transitions between two very different eras, the world's teachers find themselves caught between two very different concepts of what education and teaching should be. On the one side is the academic system from our past that currently dominates the world, but that most acknowledge is becoming less and less effective and applicable for the future. On the other side is the newly emerging alternative education in which kids are more respected and trusted, and become educated by doing and accomplishing real projects that make the world a better place—bettering themselves in the process.

THE IRONY

The irony behind the struggle, is that just as more and more teachers begin to realize that the academic education from the past is no longer appropriate for our young people's future, many of them are being pushed, by administrators as well as parents, to get better at traditional academic teaching (that is, at providing content). Most of the quality evaluations of our current educational systems are based on how well teachers do this, and how well the kids take it in. This is a big problem, and it is enormously frustrating for those teachers who see their kids needing something different and feel prevented, by "the system," from giving it to them. ("Is what I teach really what my kids need to know?" tweeted one teacher.) More and more teachers, in the terms we used in the last chapter, feel "impaled" on the cusp between two educational worlds.

Of course, there is nothing inherently wrong with either content itself or providing it—there are many instances where people being given content is appropriate and useful. But what is important to understand is that *providing content—particularly by direct instruction in classrooms—is not the only way to educate kids.* In fact, direct instruction of content is already fading as the primary means of delivering K–12 education. In our quickly evolving and technology-enabled world, "content" as it used to be thought of, is becoming incorporated and subsumed in a new vision of teaching—that of coaching and empowering kids to accomplish. In this new vision, content and instruction come only when and as needed, and from many sources, including, in addition to teachers, from technology, and, knowledgeable peers. As we move into the future, the job of full-time content provider is starting to become less mainstream and more marginal—just as the jobs of blacksmith or horse merchant did when our primary mode of transportation switched from horses to automobiles. It is already clear that in the future teachers will do something quite different in the time they spend with their students.

WHERE TEACHING IS HEADING: EMPOWERING KIDS TO BETTER THEIR WORLD

Fortunately, for both teachers and for all of us, as academic education is obsolescing in the world an alternative education is emerging. What is coming is not just a "better version of the old academics," with updated classes, content, and instruction, but rather an education based on students' understanding that they can accomplish real things in the world—things they passionately care about—by completing, as students, projects that make their world a better place, locally and globally. As noted previously, in addition to just effective thinking, this emerging education also encompasses effective action, Relationships, and Accomplishment.

Better Their World teaching is based on empowering kids to achieve in the world, rather than merely providing them with content. It has the dual benefit of not just improving kids as individuals—in more ways than now—but also of improving their world immediately in the process. Because of this, Better Their World education is growing in the world and is highly likely, in the long run, to triumph.

TEACHERS AS "EMPOWERERS"

The world now requires far more empowered kids, who can each accomplish and improve their world in their own way, and far fewer kids with particular prescribed content in their heads. What the world needs going forward is *not* kids who have learned what is already known, *not* kids who have mastered only a narrow set of thinking skills (however important), and not even kids who have "learned to learn". What the world needs are kids who have, through their own efforts, as a result of their K–12 education, and with the help of teachers, peers, and technology, figured out how to accomplish effectively and apply their passion to bettering the world. And to get there, our kids need a new and different sort of help from teachers than just the academic content and skills we provide through our current teaching.

EVOLVING INTO THE NEW ROLE OF COACH AND EMPOWERER

So emerging in the world today is a new meaning for the term "teacher," and a new kind of teaching profession. If "content (and sometimes skills) provider" was the meaning of teacher in the past, "coach and empowerer" is the new meaning of what a teacher will be in the future. As the world's education evolves toward a new model and paradigm, the world's teacher corps will gradually—hopefully sooner rather than later—let go of the content provider role, and prepare for and embrace the empowerer role.

It is unlikely that the content provider job, and the academic education that supports it, will ever *completely* go away—little in the world ever does. But the switchover, I believe, has already started. It is now in its early stages, and the most forward-thinking teachers have already evolved into empowerers. And although the evolution feels to some teachers like "jumping off a cliff" (as one described it), many have discovered that (as another who has done it assured), "the parachute opened."

Some new teachers, in fact, are already starting out their careers as empowerers and not content providers. They have found particular schools, school systems, administrators, and parents who support them in doing this, and the number of both these teachers and their supporters is growing. Some schools and administrators are already looking to hire empowerers as their teachers. Many existing teachers are embracing the new role, and already teach by supporting and guiding their students, as these empowered kids search out and find the problems that they want to solve in the world, develop the needed expertise, and marshal the resources to solve them. We may soon see the day when school administrators start advertising for "empowering teachers" separately, encouraging the changeover.

HARD QUESTIONS

Today, in addition to all the issues they have always had to deal with, all teachers must ask themselves: "How do I equip myself and grow my skills to be a part of the evolution taking place in education, and teaching?"

"Should I (and can I) move from a primary role of content provider to empowerer?" "Do I want to?" "How can I go about changing?" "Where do I find models to emulate?" "Can I blend providing content and empowering together in my teaching, or are they separate roles? In fact, all the world's teachers are beginning to arrive at a point of major choice. Do they:

- stick with providing content and academic teaching (and possibly even get better at it, although with les and less long-term benefit for their students);
- leave the teaching profession;
- move, with the world and the kids' needs, to empowering and Education to Better Their World; or
- try to do both kinds of teaching (or to combine them)?

These are not easy questions. There is often strong pressure on teachers from administrators and parents to stick with traditional academic teaching, and to do it even more strictly. But there is also increasing pressure on teachers, in more and more instances, from below, from students clamoring for something better.

Let me attempt to offer a perspective.

TWO DIFFERENT KINDS OF TEACHING:
NOT "BLENDED" BUT POSSIBLY, FOR NOW, IN PARALLEL

As the ends of education begin to shift from individual achievement to real-world accomplishment, and as we want our teachers to be ready to prepare our kids for their future, we would do best, I believe, to articulate two separate and distinct "kinds" of teaching—as well as a path for helping teachers transition from one kind to the other.

The first kind of teaching, traditional teaching, is what most teachers know how to do and do every day—our current academic teaching model. The academic teacher's primary objective—as a recent new teacher moving over from business was recently told, in no uncertain terms—is to provide content. Its goals are to get students to learn the content, and its means are various methods of content delivery (Pedagogies). Whatever the pedagogy an academic teacher employs—whether with technology or without—their job is to get their students to learn a predetermined curriculum of knowledge and/or skills. Academic teachers are constantly striving to improve how they provide their content, and their schools are constantly trying to measure how much of it has been learned by each student, and by classes as a whole.

The second kind of teaching, empowerment teaching, is a completely different process. Its ends are not to have students learn any specific, pre-specified content at any given moment. It is rather a process of empowering students to become good, effective, and world-improving people as they better their world through real, world-improving projects. Its means is not content delivery, but rather, coaching students to real-world accomplishment. The teacher's job in empowering is to give students "agency," that is, to empower students to—on their own initiative—apply their passions to doing something that the students already want to do (and are already capable of at some level), and to direct their students' efforts to improve their local and/or global world. There is a broad underlying set of skills to be acquired along the way by every student, but in Education to Better Their World this happens in a different way, in a different order, and at different times for each individual.

Empowering teaching requires a totally different set of activities and beliefs on a teacher's part than content delivery.

Of course, most of the world's teachers are already effective, to a greater or lesser degree, at content delivery. But, increasingly, there are today more and more examples of effective empowering teachers. Teachers may become good at either kind of teaching, and possibly do both: The same teacher may, already today, do content providing during the school day, and empowerment in after-school activities they conduct. It is certainly possible for the two kinds of teaching to be done within a single school—either by different teachers, or alternately by the same teacher.

NOT BOTH AT ONCE

But it is impossible, I believe, for one teacher to do content delivery and empowering *at the same time*. To ask teachers to deliver content in an empowering way (e.g., by letting go of control) or to ask them to empower kids by instructing them on content, is futile. It will only lead to frustration and failure.

It is not a "blend" that teachers should be after but a *choice* at any given moment. It is far easier, I believe, for teachers to move from content provider to empowerer (and perhaps back again) if they see these as two separate kinds of teaching—not skills to be blended together or done simultaneously. That way, they can know precisely what they are doing and are expected to do at any given moment. Otherwise they, and all of us, will be enormously confused and frustrated—which is pretty much the current state of things. (Some do speak of a "blended system" as one in which academic teaching is done some of the time and empowering teaching at other times. That can work, but it is different from doing them both at once.)

Of course, when one person does two different jobs, the two don't always get done equally or equally well; one of the jobs often gets favored, or preferred, over the other. But people's preferences for one role over another can change over time as people become more comfortable in a new role. Many teachers who have moved on to empowering would never go back.

So I recommend that in making the transition, teachers—and all of us—think of two separate, alternative kinds of teaching. Moving from one kind to the other involves changing some fundamental attitudes about what teaching is, and—in the words of one teacher who has made the transition successfully—a lot of letting go, particularly of the kinds of strict classroom management and control of student behavior that often characterizes academic education. Some find this difficult, but not all do.

Some of this letting go has already been in process over the past 15 or 20 years—many teachers have transitioned from being what was often known as the "sage on the stage" to becoming more of a "guide on the side." This movement has involved teachers understanding how to help students to become the agents of their own learning, and leaders of their own projects. Much project-based learning (PBL) fits into this transitional category, and can be seen as a first step toward empowerment, because the students have more individual latitude and responsibility.

But in PBL, as it is currently practiced, teachers almost always guide students within a specific curriculum, to meet a set of content standards. In the new empowering role, the letting-go goes much further. There is no universally delivered content curriculum—only a set of underlying skills to be acquired by all at various times and in various ways. Teachers must put a lot more trust in students and give them far more freedom. Students learn skills and information about the world as they solve local and world problems of their own selection. In the new role the teacher throws the doors to the world wide open to students, to the world's problems, its knowledge, its resources, and its avenues to change.

Teachers who have already begun the transition need to finally evolve from "guide on the side within a curricular structure," to "empowerer where both teacher and students are liberated." The endpoint is a far looser structure, where each student is the initiator, and where the teacher supports each student's real-world problem solving with an eye to the student's development of effective thinking, action, relationships, and accomplishment skills. Teachers looking to speed this transition can try doing the different kinds of teaching on separate days of the week. My friend, teacher Esther Wojcicki (whom we will meet in a moment) has a great version of this she calls "Moonshot Mondays."

DESCRIBING THE NEW EMPOWERER ROLE

Of course before anyone chooses to move to a new job or role, they certainly want a good idea of what it involves. What, exactly, is the job of an empowerer?

The role of an empowering teacher is to enable kids at all levels to succeed at a series of successive, and increasingly challenging real, world-improving projects: projects of the kids' own choosing, projects that benefit both the world and themselves, projects that help the kids understand themselves better, projects that utilize and apply the students' passions and stretch their capabilities, and projects that lead to the students becoming good, effective, and world-improving people.

One interesting thing about this kind of teaching is that the teacher need not necessarily know very much about the "content" of the students' projects at all. An elementary school teacher coaching a team making a robot, for example, may know almost nothing at all about robotics. But she can certainly be effective at coaching the team to get all the information and expertise they need, and help them through the rough patches to accomplish their goal.

LEARNING A NEW KIND OF TEACHING

Because almost all our teachers currently do academic education—and experienced it themselves as students—to make the transition and to learn the new job of empowerer they will need to distinguish, and those supporting them will need to help them distinguish, among three things:

1. Activities that are specific to content delivery that teachers need to *discontinue* when doing the empowerer job. These activities include "direct instruction," "covering content," and "teaching, in order, a prescribed curriculum." (Empowering teachers can, of course help kids learn—mostly on their own—whatever they need in order to accomplish and complete their projects.)

2. Activities they already do that are *common to both* kinds of teaching, and that teachers need to do even more of in the empowering role. These activities include principally the behavior and attitude of the teacher toward the students. Empowering teacher Esther Wojcicki (who invented "Moonshot Mondays" and about whom we will hear more shortly) has captured these skills nicely in her acronym T.R.I.C.K. It stands for Trust, Respect, Independence, Collaboration, and Kindness. These behaviors are helpful, of course, for any teacher, but without them, empowering is impossible. To the extent that academic teachers already do these things while delivering content, they should continue to do them while empowering. For teachers who currently employ less trust, respect, independence, collaboration, and kindness toward students in their academic teaching, becoming an empowering teacher will be harder and will involve more change.

3. Activities that are specific to empowering—new activities that every teacher who does that job needs to learn and master. These include helping kids find and do projects that fit their strengths and interests and allow them to deeply apply their passion(s). They include coaching their students to follow through to the end and complete their projects, to get the help and feedback they need along the way, and to understand what they have gained from doing them. They include knowing what projects and roles will help individual kids develop and stretch their capabilities. They include letting kids progress at their own speed as long as they are headed toward the proper goal, even if there are numerous missteps and failures along the way. They include building the skills not just of effective thinking, but in addition, the skills of effective action, Effective Relationships, and effective accomplishment as they do their projects.

Empowerer is very much a new job for an academic, content-providing teacher to learn how to do.

SOME EMPOWERERS I'VE MET

Many teachers, though, have already learned how to do it. I know—and know of—many empowering teachers in the world. Only a relative few today, however, do the empowering job full time. One teacher who does, and who has been doing the empowering job for a long time (and who is one of the very best at it), is Esther Wojcicki.

Esther has taught English and journalism at Palo Alto High School ("Paly"), in Palo Alto, California—the same town that hosts Stanford University—for 31 years. Now, in what may be her final full-time teaching year, she works in a beautiful, new, custom-built facility known as the Media Arts Center. But for almost all of her years as a teacher, Esther taught in what is known as a "temporary"—one large, dank room in what I would call a Quonset hut. When Esther taught there, that room was stuffed to the brim with up to 80 students at a time, plus all the many newspapers and magazines those students read and produced.

It's important to hear Esther speak in her own words about her work, and there are numerous videos online on her website (www. moonshotsedu.com) and elsewhere, where she does so. Esther recently published a book about her teaching entitled *Moonshots in Education* (Wojcicki, 2015)[33] in which she discusses her methodology and results. Testimonies to the efficacy of her work come in continually from her former students. My favorite is this comment from the actor James Franco, one of Esther's best-known former students: "She showed me I could take my dreams as seriously as I wanted."

That is what an empowering teacher does—that is at its core, that is what empowerment is.

A second teacher whose empowering work I will highlight is Jenny Henry, who teaches fifth grade—also in a public school—in Douglas County, Colorado. Jenny was for many years a traditional, content-providing teacher, frustrated, as are many teachers, by the academic system and how it was not allowing her kids to flourish as much as she thought they could. So Jenny spent a summer thinking hard about what to do, emerging in the fall as an empowerer—letting and helping her students do world-improving projects as a big part of their education. I watched Jennie and her highly supportive superintendent at that time,

Dr. Elizabeth Fagan, proudly bring kids up on stage to describe the robot "controller" they designed and built to help a disabled student attend and participate in classes from his bed. Jennie is the teacher who tells all her colleagues, "Jump off the cliff—the parachute will open." And, she also tells them, "It only took me a summer to change."

The third empowerer I will mention is not a teacher but rather a senior administrator who works closely hand-in-hand with his teachers. David Engle, who recently retired as Superintendent of Schools in Port Townsend, WA, after a career of successful administrative roles in a number of other places, tells all his teachers this: "I want all your kids to be doing real-world projects. But before I approve any project, you need to show me how it will benefit the community." David has spent his entire career building strong relations between schools and local communities, and encouraging students to become involved in doing local projects. He cites the ability of his approach to reach "lost" kids—such as a "totally disengaged" kid he watched find his passion in the engine room of an old boat the kid was restoring for the community.

It is worth highlighting that the three people I just mentioned all work in public schools and not in independent private schools—many of which have been doing service projects for a long time and are already moving in more empowering directions.

WHY WOULD A TEACHER BECOME AN EMPOWERER? WHAT'S IN IT FOR THEM?

Just about all today's current teachers are content providers, and many are already good or great at it. They know how to do what is required of them in traditional teaching—that is, deliver content, control their classes, and raise students' "outcomes" (defined as grades and graduation rates). What do these academic teachers think of the new job of empowerer? Will they want to learn to do it?

Some, of course, will resist and decline to take the path to the future—they will continue providing content to those kids and parents who want it for the rest of their teaching careers. There may be nothing we can do to influence these people other than showing them the happier kids and parents who result from empowering, and letting them hear from colleagues who have changed. But they should understand that their kids will suffer from being stuck with an academics-only education—if not in terms of grades, in terms of being truly prepared for their future.

My strong sense, though, is that a great many current academic teachers will be quite pleased, thankful that they are given the opportunity to move forward. There are a great many teachers today who are frustrated with just providing content, and are anxious to do something more beneficial for their kids. There are also many younger people entering the teaching profession who don't want to repeat what was done—and done to them—in the past. Many are looking for a new route. Empowering kids to better their world is a very different job from providing content and improving kids' performance on tests. Empowering is a job that I believe is attractive to a great many teachers in the world.

And for some teachers, the change will be nothing new. There are already many teachers who—even though they know they are in the academic system—already see themselves as empowerers. We just met some of them. "My life's passion and work," says Esther Wojcicki, "has been to 'empower' kids in a variety of settings, situations, and relationships." Many teachers in technology roles already see their job as empowering students (and other teachers). For people such as these who have already made the move in thought and/or in practice, specifying and naming a new teaching job of empowerer will be a welcome move toward the future. These teachers are already seeking out schools and administrators who will support them in their quest.

And let us not forget our education schools and in-service programs. These need to also begin to shift quickly from teaching content providing to teaching empowering. Although education schools tend to be conservative, some, like Stanford University in California, are already looking in these new directions. The earlier the alternative of empowerer enters our teacher preparation and in-service programs, and the earlier people go into teaching because they want to empower kids, the better it will be. I and others will certainly be looking to promote change here.

INCENTIVES TO CHANGE

One of the most unfortunate things about our traditional academic education is what it has done to many of the people who chose to become teachers. Being a content provider and "academic achievement improver" in these changing times has turned far too many of these individuals from innovative, well-meaning people who truly want to help kids, into rule and curriculum followers who fear losing their jobs should they dare to do what they know is right for their kids.

Making changes, though, takes effort, and people generally need incentives to put forth that effort—that is, their effort needs to bring them, either in the short or the long term, something they value. Like most of us, teachers value—among other things—job satisfaction, comfort, and monetary rewards. And also like most of us, they are not averse to putting forth effort beyond their daily jobs to achieve those things. Since academic teaching typically offers more pay to teachers with higher degrees, a great many teachers continue their education while they teach.

Could moving to the empowerer job potentially raise teachers' pay as well? While this is by no means clear, an Education to Better Their World improves the world in real and measurable ways. As the world sees value-adding improvements emerging from its educational investments in Better Their World education, one can speculate that we may begin to value those teachers more highly and pay them more. Already, the salaries of teachers in some experimental private schools are higher than average—those places may already be paying more for good, empowering teachers.

Whether teachers' salaries will go up as education moves from content providing to empowerment is, of course, speculation at this point, of course. But just continuing to assert that our teachers are "worth more than they are paid" has not proven to be an effective argument for raising their salaries. Because empowered kids can actually add value to the world, the case for teachers' getting paid more to empower kids rather than to provide them with content may be an easier one to make.

There would also be strong incentive for teachers to embrace empowering if it made their work life easier. Would learning and taking on the new role of empowerer do this? The answer to that is almost certainly "yes"—but, it must be clear, only in the longer term and after a good deal of effort has been put in. Learning to do any new job takes work; it is not easy for most. But once the initial stages of that work are done, doing the teaching job as an empowerer *is* easier than doing it as a content provider. Not standing in front of the class "telling" for hours every day, not marking papers every day, not preparing daily lesson plans, frees up a lot of time. There are many other things that empowerers need to do with that time of course, but many teachers will see them as less onerous.

A third incentive to change—and for many this may be the biggest—is increased job satisfaction, that is, making one's work life more interesting, exciting, and "spiritually" rewarding. Becoming an empowering teacher will almost certainly do this. Coaching kids to accomplish projects the kids themselves have initiated, and to which they are fully applying their passions, is far more interesting, exciting, rewarding, and enjoyable than struggling to get kids to embrace a subject they may not care about. Helping and seeing kids accomplish projects that actually improve their world—and seeing the kids' confidence increase as they do—is far more satisfying, for most teachers, than seeing their kids raise their grades by a few points. A big part of the increased job satisfaction that comes from being an empowering teacher, moreover, comes from the fact that the job of empowerer is truly—far more than the role of content provider—a job that will improve the world, in ways that can be seen and felt immediately.

THE BEST ARGUMENT FOR CHANGE

Because our best teachers have always been those who care the most deeply about their kids and their kids' real needs, perhaps the best argument of all for teachers' becoming empowering teachers is that our kids truly require it.

In the future, any student who has *not* acquired as a result of his or her education an understanding of how to apply their unique mix of skills to positive real-world accomplishment, who does *not* have a history of real-world accomplishment, who has *not* mastered, in addition to disciplined thinking skills, the action, relationship, and accomplishment skills that are needed to succeed in the future, who has *not* become the kind of good, capable, world-improving person required by the institutions and world of the future, and who has *not* become symbiotic with our new world of technology, is unlikely to succeed—no matter how much academic math, language arts, science, and social studies content they may have been instructed in, and learned.

How can we, as educators, *not* meet this need? As citizens, we cannot let this need for change in our education—and in how our teachers deliver it—jeopardize the future of our society, our kids, and our people. If we, as a society, allow all our teachers to deliver the same kind of academic, content-based education they have been doing up until now—even if they have been doing it all their lives and do it extremely well—all our people, kids and adults, will suffer immensely. It is not even enough to argue that content and academic education may help kids get into college and succeed in the short term. Even if that is still the case for the moment, it will very soon not be. Education and teachers must adapt to the new world by becoming empowerers, and to do so quickly.

HOW TO BECOME AN EMPOWERER

Suppose you—or any teacher—wants to move from being a content provider to being an empowerer. What can and should you do? What steps should you take?

Fortunately, there are new groups emerging to help teachers in making the transition. One of these is Esther Wojcicki's *MoonshotsEDU* (www.moonshotsedu.com).

If you are a teacher and it is your desire to go in this direction, you must of course be realistic about the fact that there are likely to be barriers to overcome. But knowing what those barriers are will help you to more easily get over them.

First, you will almost certainly have to fight against conventional educational wisdom. If you are currently a traditional academic teacher you have likely been instructed, from day one, that your primary job—no matter what you think your kids need, or what your personal philosophy of helping kids might be— is to deliver content. You were probably also told, as academic teachers typically are, that your other key tasks are (2) classroom management (i.e. making sure the kids are quietly working on whatever tasks they have been assigned), and (3) improving outcomes, (i.e. making sure their kids get better grades). More recently academic teachers are also being told that they need to put more focus on skills, defined mostly as "disciplined thinking skills." But there is a lot more to education than this conventional wisdom, and you will need to be clear in your mind that *your* goal for students is accomplishment.

A second barrier you may have to overcome is peer and administrative pressure. Many new teachers with "different" ideas are, through various means, pressured into conformity during their initial teaching years. We need to create more networks and support systems to help teachers resist this pressure. Fortunately, technology can help a lot with this—online support groups of empowering teachers are already forming around the world.

An third barrier to teachers moving to empowering is that many, perhaps even most, teachers who see and feel the mismatch feel powerless to make changes. I see this far too often, particularly in public

K–12 schools—the issue of teachers' perceived powerlessness in the face of "the system" comes up in just about every place and country where I speak. Anywhere I go in the world, a teacher will inevitably ask: "Yes, I see the need for change, and I agree with many of your ideas, but what can I do? I'm given a curriculum to teach and I have to teach it." There are far too many of these "Yes . . . buts" unnecessarily in teachers' heads. I believe teachers, in general, are far more powerful than many of them believe.

A final barrier you will certainly have to overcome is pressure from parents. Too many parents today are fearful that educational change will harm, rather than help their kids, and this can be an intimidating barrier as well.

So what is a forward-thinking teacher to do? We need to find ways to overcome these barriers. Fortunately, there are some.

OVERCOMING THE BARRIERS

The first, I believe, is recognizing that "content provider" and "empowerer" are very different roles. This means that a content provider who wants to become an empowerer needs to do (at least) three big things:

First, they need to learn the skills and role of empowerer—that is, what it is and all it entails. This can be facilitated, to a certain extent, through seminars and websites. Hopefully, undergraduate and graduate education schools will soon begin offering preparation in empowering as well. (It is, of course, ironic to have 'academic courses" in "empowering." This dilemma will need to be gradually worked out.)

Second, any teacher who wants to change to empowering needs to find at least one administrator to support them in their new teaching approach—it is much, much harder, and sometimes impossible, to do this in an unsupported way. Fortunately, such administrators do exist— principals, heads of school, even superintendents—you just met one: David Engle. It may in extreme cases take a change of school to find the right supporting administrator, but it is almost certainly worth it.

Third, a teacher who wants to be an empowerer needs to practice. Esther Wojcicki suggests "putting a toe in the water," by doing the new job *alternatively* with the old one on different days. She suggests letting kids do projects one day a week, with the teacher in the empowerer role. It is likely that almost any teacher, after appropriate conversations with students, administrators (and possibly parents) can begin a program where students are empowered to do real-world projects—in their class time—for a single day every week. This idea is similar to, and inspired by the "20 percent" time that Google offers its employees to do their own, personal projects. Esther found that her students strongly prefer to do this kind of day at the beginning of the week than at the end, so she calls her version "Moonshot Mondays." Students can then continue their projects out of class as much as they want to, and can look forward to not just one "different" day during the year, but to an empowering day every week. Esther is currently creating a set of suggestions and plans for how to implement her approach in a way that allows for a lot of experimentation and still leaves time for content delivery.

An even more radical approach, of course, is for a teacher who wants to be an empowerer to find a new teaching job at a school whose goal *already is* to empower its students. Today, new private schools are being started all over the world with student empowerment as their goal and with real, world-improving, project-based education in mind. Even the historically traditional International Baccalaureate schools are adding more projects and empowerment to their Primary and Middle School programs; "Education for a Better World" is currently their website tagline. Many public charter schools are doing more real-world projects (e.g., High Tech High in San Diego). And more and more true public schools are moving in these directions, both in the United States (e.g., Port Townsend, WA) and around the world, (e.g., Dreamdo schools, based in Finland).

One of the salient features of our new world is that people change jobs more frequently—and that includes people changing out of the teaching profession. Because of this change, and retirement, a high percentage of teachers formed in the previous generation will, by many estimates, no longer be teaching in the next. Although we don't want to lose all continuity with the past, this huge turnover presents us with an enormous opportunity for the future. The best way to *waste* this opportunity would be to allow all or most of our new and remaining teachers to remain only content providers, and for them to try to do better what we have always done—perhaps now with the help of technology. The best way to *use* this opportunity would be to lead our remaining and future teachers toward empowering and Education to Better Their World.

It is unlikely that many schools, or teachers will switch plans completely overnight. But it would be enormously useful if every place responsible for education (country, state, district) undertook a program to create a future teacher corps of empowerers, and did so quickly, incorporating the full Better Their World education, including its new ends (Bettering Their World), its new means (Real, world-improving accomplishment), its new supporting curriculum (of Effective Thinking, Effective Action, Effective Relationships, and Effective Accomplishment), and its new teaching job (empowering), along with the powerful use of emerging technology.

It is crucial that these new paradigms and ideas be introduced at the start of teachers' education and professional development—we can no longer let our teachers base their future work on the kind of teaching they received as students. Once this is done new teachers can—in a reversal—mentor experienced ones, sharing what they both know. Students must also be brought, early on, into the conversation about how to best educate for the future (many of the new ideas in this book have come from them.) Politicians and administrators must be clear that it is this new approach and paradigm of education—and not the old one— that will help their economic development in the longer term. Educators and politicians must work together to provide a path for current teachers to become retrained and recertified in the "empowerment to better their world" approach.

As quickly as teachers are trained to fill them, countries and districts should create new schools based on the new paradigms. They should present these schools to the public in a way that makes parents compete to get their kids in, and in a manner that makes kids fight to attend. Creating a new type of public school *is* possible—it has happened in the United States with charter schools (although, sadly, most of what those schools offer is still a variation of the old academic education), and in other places as well.

Our job must now be to get everyone—teachers, kids, parents, and politicians—excited about moving to the new, empowering, Better Their World education as soon as possible. Or it will take far too long to get there—to our kids' and the world's loss.

CHAPTER 12

Will Change Happen?

MANY ARE PESSIMISTIC about change coming to education, but I am an optimist. I believe a new kind of education is coming sooner rather than later, because it is so necessary and the roadmap is already becoming clear.

ENORMOUS FRUSTRATION

The world has become enormously frustrated with its current education system. Having spent huge amounts of effort trying to spread academic education to more and more young people around the globe—and succeeding for a time in many (though certainly not all) cases—academic education now appears to be working less successfully than before and losing much of the power that it once had to improve the world and people's lives. Most recognize the world is changing, and most think that education ought to adapt to it, and yet, despite huge efforts on the part of many, fundamental change in education seems to be slow and often nonexistent. Some still vociferously oppose our education's changing at all, seeing our current system as a bulwark of our success in the past. A great many wonder whether meaningful change will *ever* come to the world's K–12 education on a massive scale.

Will the world's primary and secondary education *ever* switch to a new educational model that takes account of our new context and kids' capabilities? Can we help make this happen? Or is the best we can do in our lifetimes to just continue to make incremental improvements to the academic education of the past—as many are now doing—that are less effective than we hope? This is a huge issue on a great many people's minds, some of whom have already spent (and, in some cases, wasted or lost) large fortunes on this problem. Certainly, there is a great deal of time and energy being spent on educational change.

WHAT'S BEEN MISSING

I believe a big piece has been missing up until now in almost all our discussions of educational change—something that only a relative few have, as yet, realized. As we come to the end of this discussion and book, I want to clarify and highlight this missing element:

What has been lacking, up to this point, is a shared vision of what a different K–12 education for the future should look like.

It's a lot easier for someone to say, "I don't want A anymore" if there is a clear alternative B to go to. If the alternative to today's academic education is a clear vision of a better place where many already want to go, it is far easier to help them all get there. Up until recently that common alternative vision did not exist in the world—there were only scattered, partial, and individual alternative visions. What I am now observing is that, in an adaptive response to the world's big contextual changes, a common vision is now stating to emerge in its broad outlines, and is beginning to coalesce in various people's minds and into specific initiatives. So I have focused my attention—and tried to focus yours—on that missing and emerging vision.

WHAT CAUSES CHANGE?

Massive social change—other than that caused by cataclysmic events—has typically happened gradually. Elements of the context shift, and people very slowly adapt. What are eventually seen as massive changes generally begin on the margins, with individuals and small groups, and slowly gather adherents, success, and momentum until a "tipping point" is reached.

Anthropologist Margaret Mead famously remarked: "Never doubt that a small group of thoughtful, committed citizens can change the world; indeed, it's the only thing that ever has." Today in education we see a great many such "small groups of thoughtful concerned citizens" out there, each trying to change education in its own way. And at the same time, we see a huge speedup in the pace at which many changes have occurred in our times—with the sorts of cultural shifts that used to take centuries or decades now often happening, often abetted by technology, in a matter of years.

So, will change come to K–12 education? And if so, how rapidly? We all know there is great resistance to change from many quarters, but is meaningful change already starting to emerge? In some ways—despite everyone's frustrations—we may be further along in the change process than we think, because there are commonalities in a great many of the change efforts that are now happening inside and outside of schools. As a result, there is emerging a new "model" of what K–12 education should be, a model that differs in several fundamental ways from today's ubiquitous academic K–12 education. But up until now, that new model of a fundamentally different education has never been clearly identified, named, or generally understood. That is the contribution I hope to make with this book.

THE "FORMULA FOR CHANGE"

There exists in the world a simple formula for assessing the likely success of organizational change programs. It was created in the early 1960s, by David Gleicher while he was working at Arthur D. Little[34] and refined by Kathie Dannemiller in the 1980s.[35] It is often known as the "formula for change." It is not, of course, a formula in the scientific sense of a law of nature that always works, but rather a model—that is, an abstract, highly simplified and somewhat metaphorical perspective on what causes change to happen. It is far from the only model of change. Some, perhaps, consider it simplistic, but I believe that applying this model to education can be useful to our thinking.

According to the model or formula, *even when* there is great dissatisfaction with the present state, and *even when* most agree change is sorely needed, two other elements, in addition to the dissatisfaction must be present for change to actually happen. Change only happens, says the model, and the natural human resistance to change can be overcome, *only when the combination of three factors*, including:

- *Dissatisfaction* with how things are

combined with

- a common *Vision* of what is possible (i.e., of a better future) combined with

- some *First concrete steps* taken toward the vision

is greater than the resistance to change.

Put into a quasi-mathematical form, change only happens when

$$D \times V \times F > R$$

where D is Dissatisfaction, V is Vision, F is First steps, and R is Resistance to change. Multiplication of the formula's factors means that if any one factor is absent, the product is zero and the resistance to change will not be overcome.

APPLYING THE FORMULA

I think we can all agree that the R, the *resistance to change in education*, is high and difficult to overcome. I will not dwell on this. But can the formula help us to understand what, if anything, is standing in the way of overcoming that resistance? Let's examine each term.

DISSATISFACTION

I think we can say with some certainty that dissatisfaction with our current K–12 education is high and growing. We see students expressing their dissatisfaction in polls, online videos,[36] and especially through nonparticipation (a combination of not engaging and dropping out). We see teachers expressing dissatisfaction through their blogs and unions, and through leaving the profession by retiring or resigning. We see administrators expressing dissatisfaction through their continuous support of new pilots, and frequent turnover. We see politicians expressing dissatisfaction through their many calls for reform. We see philanthropists and capitalists expressing dissatisfaction through their large investments in change. We see many, if not most, books, articles, and lectures on education around the world now starting by acknowledging this dissatisfaction. We see—despite some real successes of a relatively small number of kids, teachers, schools, and perhaps even one or two countries in the world—that more and more of our students are less and less engaged. We see schools considered "failing," because their students are not making the progress we seek in our measurements. We see key skills our kids need not being taught or learned. We see support and money for education often lacking. We see reforms that help but don't scale. We see new programs and technologies that do the same old things over and over in new ways. Our mainstream education just doesn't evolve. The list of frustrations with education is seemingly endless. So I think we can stipulate that the term D: *Dissatisfaction* is high and growing.

What about the other factors?

FIRST STEPS

Despite the fact that the majority of so-called education reforms are nothing but incremental changes to our old system, in recent years growing numbers of "first steps" to something better have begun to emerge in the world. These are schools, and ideas, that demonstrate in diverse ways what various parts of a new and better education model could and should look like. Among these first steps are some of the things being done in poorer countries around the world (e.g., in Vicky Colbert's Escuela Nueva schools). They include some schools in the United States, including certain "charter" schools, (e.g., High Tech High in San Diego, Summit Public Schools in Silicon Valley), and some U.S. public school systems (e.g., Port Townsend, WA, and Douglas County, CO). First steps include some brand new schools starting up around the world (e.g., AltSchool and XQ in Silicon Valley). They include some long-existing private school programs, such as many International Baccalaureate school "service" programs. They include individual real-world project programs within public and private schools. They include individual teachers making changes in their own classrooms. They include proposed curricular changes such as the "character" and "whole person" education movements.

At this time, little brings all these first steps together. But the point at this moment is *not* what the details of these first steps are, it is rather that there *are* many first steps beyond academic education, in really new directions. Many of these are still in the planning stage, or just getting started. My focus here is not on the details (the next volume will detail many of them) but on their number. What seems to be clear is that the third term in the change formula, F: *First steps*, is a positive (and growing) number.

SHARED VISION—THE MISSING ELEMENT

What I want to focus more and particular attention on is the "middle" term of the formula, V: *the Vision of what is possible*. It is this vision that I believe has been sorely absent in many current discussions of education reform—which is why so many of those reforms turn out to be merely incremental accretions to our current academic education.

What the world has sorely lacked—and this may have been, up until now, *the* major barrier in the way of our making faster and more substantive educational progress—is *a new common vision*, or paradigm, of what a K–12 education could and should be in our future and new times. Because if the formula is right—and that common vision term is missing (and therefore zero)—change will not happen until it arrives. So I believe it will be extremely helpful if we all get a clearer understanding of the key elements of the vision that is emerging, and how that new vision, model, and paradigm differs fundamentally from the education of the past.

I have tried to provide an outline of that vision in this book. I have tried to specify not just its ends (bettering their world), but also its means (real-world accomplishment), its desired outcomes (people who are effective thinkers, actors, relators, and accomplishers in areas they are passionate about) and how our teachers, and a new and more powerful use of technology can help get us there.

This emerging new vision is starting to become clearer. This raises the middle term of the change formula—the V or "common vision" term—from zero to a positive number. Combined with the other two terms that are high or growing, this means—hopefully—that the resistance to change will be overcome, and that change is more likely to occur, and more quickly.

One thing this emerging vision still lacks, and needs badly, is a commonly-agreed-upon name—short, simple, and memorable—so that people can say, "I don't want an academic education for myself (or for my kid), I want '___' instead." We are still searching for that name. I have suggested "Education to Better Their World," and "Real-world Accomplishment-Based Education" as candidates. There will be other suggestions (I have heard "Agency-Based Education") and one of them will, I am sure, eventually catch on.

NECESSARY, BUT NOT SUFFICIENT

We must be clear, though, that a new vision by itself is not sufficient to cause everyone—or even anyone—to change. Another useful saying is that, *"People do not change when they see the light, they change when they feel the heat."* We are talking here about massive social change, and it will take some time—possibly decades, maybe more—and much "heat" no doubt as well, for it to fully happen. But it bears remembering that a key characteristic of our current age is accelerating change. Today, change often takes us by surprise by happening far more quickly than it did in the past—many are amazed, for example, by how quickly the online world, and so many of the things it enables, have grown. Having a shared vision is an important step, I believe, in helping educational change happen faster.

NOT "TOP DOWN"

It is unlikely, however, that *any* vision in our current world will be shared because it is proclaimed, directed, or adopted formally from above. That was often how things worked in the past, but it is unlikely to work today. We now have, with our new technologies and connections, a new and powerful "bottom-up" force in the world. Today's shared visions emerge from the bottom-up practices of all the groups doing things differently, *in combination with* new ideas from above. And that is what is happening. I'm not inventing this emerging vision. I'm just documenting and curating it.

And because *without* a shared vision change is unlikely to overcome the resistance, it is terribly important that we all *do* understand the new vision of education and, hopefully, "see the light," so we can decide together how much of it is indeed "common" and work collectively to make it more so.

CHAPTER 13

What People Can Do

IN CHAPTER 1, I wrote that I hoped readers of this book would include "government leaders and politicians, educational policy makers, parents, educational innovators at all levels, current and aspiring superintendents, school administrators and principals, graduate students of urban government and educational policy, teachers and teacher educators, members of the general public interested in and invested in providing children with the right education for our present and their future—and especially young people." Now, near the end of the book, I'd like to offer suggestions for some actions that readers from each of these groups who are interested in advancing the emerging vision I have described can (and hopefully will) take.

GOVERNMENT LEADERS AND POLITICIANS

Most leaders and politicians in the world today see education as important to their country's development—poorer countries see it as a way of catching up, richer ones as a way of remaining near the top. If you are a leader you must understand, and, importantly, act on the understanding that *it is moving to the new* Better Their World *education—and not just shoring up the old academic approach—that will help your country's economic development in the longer term*. Far too few leaders and politicians support anything other than incremental change, but the time for massive updating of our education is upon us. Now is the perfect time for visionary politicians who care about the future, and about our kids, to open up the debate—widely, in public, and with a high profile—between the educational needs of citizens educated in the past and the educational needs of those citizens' kids' for the future. A huge opportunity for leadership lays within these politicians' grasp: those that speed its progress along will be rewarded and long remembered.

My guess is that some smaller country will be the first to sufficiently see the light (and feel the heat) and, by moving quickly to a real-world, accomplishment-based "Education to Better Their World," system, will move their students not only ahead, but have them leapfrog the world. A wonderful long-term educational goal for such a country would be to have "every citizen become a world-class accomplisher at whatever they love to do." Now is the moment to seize this huge political and social opportunity.

BUSINESS, GOVERNMENT AND NGO LEADERS

Business, government and nongovernmental organization (NGO) leaders who are unhappy with the results from our current academic education systems are now able to do more than just complain about public education or start their own educational tracks. They can also get their organizations to begin formulating real-world projects for students to do, at all grade levels—projects that actually help their organizations and the world—and begin submitting them (via processes to be created) to the schools and kids. Imagine every company having an employee responsible for collecting, formulating, and submitting projects to schools, and for collecting and using the results. Imagine parallel teams of kids working on company, government and NGO projects all over the world, under "credit" and/or "fair, performance-based compensation" schemes to be determined. How much value could our kids potentially add to the world?

EDUCATIONAL POLICY MAKERS

Educational policy makers can and must begin opening up their thinking to very different alternative possibilities for the future. Forward-thinking educational policy is no longer about teaching the MESS better, or raising standards, or adding more STE(A)M courses, or incorporating the Internet and technology into our existing programs—all of which does little more than restructure the past. The U.S.'s Common Core, for example, took decades of effort to develop and roll out—effort that could have been much more usefully devoted to initiatives far more oriented to the future. Any forward-looking educational policy must be about creating new and more effective means of empowering our kids to better their world, and the formulation of such policies ought to include far more bottom-up participation by kids. Policies need to include strong support for teaching as empowering, so that our teachers feel free to experiment and change. Policy makers must look more carefully at which measurements actually matter for individual kids, and back away from our current unhelpful over-reliance on—and fixation with—numerical comparisons, and data that do not really measure education. The future requires a new and different education; policy makers can, and hopefully will, create the path for getting there.

PARENTS

Parents today are caught in what often seems a very tough bind. On the one hand they all want the best for their kids—which to them often means "the best education available when they grew up." But they also see the world changing, old jobs disappearing, and their kids wanting different things—and they know, at some level, that the world they themselves grew up in no longer exists. What today's parents need, more than anything else is the courage to help their kids move ahead in a new world and environment that is unfamiliar and for which their own experience provides little useful guidance. Parents need to be helped to understand that success in the old academic system, while still useful, is in many cases less important than it was in the past; today academic success is not the only—or even necessarily the best—path for every kid. To truly help their kids, parents need to emphasize far more the kinds of real-world accomplishments that will be important to their kids' success in the future, and far less the kinds of grades and achievements that were important in the parents' times. They need to listen hard to what their kids are telling them about the future, and work hard to help their kids find and apply their own passion—irrespective of the parents' own desires and needs. It takes a great deal of courage and effort on the part of parents to help their kids face a world that, as "digital immigrants," they do not completely understand. We all need to help parents find the courage to give their kids an education that represents the future, and not just their own past. For parents who find this courage, the rewards are great: not only the positive attitudes of their kids today, but their kids' success in the world of tomorrow.

EDUCATIONAL INNOVATORS AT ALL LEVELS

The many so-called (and often self-proclaimed) "innovators" in education today—both technological and pedagogical—divide, in my experience, into two groups. The first group, and by far the biggest (perhaps as many as 90%) innovate—if you can call it that—only within the confines of the old academic system. Many of those who start new schools—independent or charter—fall into this group, as does everyone who tries to present or deliver the MESS curriculum in new ways (e.g., via video or other technology). My sense is that this group—and most of this so-called innovation within the old academic education—will ultimately lead, despite huge investments of time energy and money, to very little long-term benefit for kids. I strongly recommend that all those who see themselves as educational innovators carefully examine whether the proposals, innovations, software, etc., that they are creating or championing serve primarily to improve the academic education of the past, or whether their innovations truly support and move us toward the real, world-improving accomplishment-based education of the future. There is a huge opportunity for innovation in moving education from the academic paradigm to the new paradigm of empowering kids to better their world. That is where all smart educational innovators should be focusing their efforts and investments, because that is where the true long-term payoff will be—both for our kids and for us.

CURRENT AND ASPIRING SUPERINTENDENTS, SCHOOL ADMINISTRATORS, AND PRINCIPALS

Individuals running our current schools, and those aspiring to run them, should be carefully and continuously looking within their own buildings and systems for emerging instances of the new paradigm that they can encourage. Administrators should be seeking out and identifying those teachers already working in the new paradigm (and those who want to), and those students who are already doing the kinds of projects we have described—in or out of school—and giving them particular support. School administrators should be seeking out ways to highlight what those students and teachers are accomplishing, and inventing new ways, such as teacher-to-teacher, student-to-teacher and school-to-parent mentoring programs, to be spreading what people have done well in their system to others—encouraging and helping everyone in their schools and districts to evolve toward the new paradigm.

Administrators looking for a place to start might begin by systematically implementing programs like Esther Wojcicki's "Moonshot Monday" idea discussed earlier. Building on the work of David Engle and others, administrators should begin tying their schools and their kids far more tightly to the real-world needs of the communities in which they are located. It is worth remembering that there are no well-defined "best-practices" to follow here; as in any evolving field there are only "good practices" and the need to invent better ones. Each administrator should become an original innovator within his or her own context.

GRADUATE STUDENTS OF URBAN GOVERNMENT AND EDUCATIONAL POLICY

The individuals now studying in our graduate schools of education are many of the people who will shape the education of the future in profound ways as they move into government and administrative positions. Most of these graduate students are from generations that are closer to today's K–12 kids than long-time educators; many of them clearly recognize the need for change and are anxious to be part of it. These individuals must realize that they are in a perfect position to start formulating and shaping the ideas and policies that will move education into the new era—this is "their time." They must be willing not just to do so, but also to push back hard against the outdated teachings of the past, whenever they are offered.

TEACHERS

Based on my constant conversations with teachers around the world, I am convinced that there are quite large numbers of teachers, almost everywhere, who want to do something different—and better—with and for their kids. What these people require more than anything else is support, and encouragement to seek that support. Teachers who feel the need for change should be continually seeking assistance from both like-minded colleagues and administrators in their own schools, and also searching online for ideas, innovative colleagues, and practical examples, all of which are growing daily. The teachers should be frequently talking with their colleagues and their students about experimentation. They should be having frequent conversations *not* about learning and grades, but about the kind education kids need. Teachers should be continuously seeking opportunities to work with students in new and better real-world accomplishment-oriented ways and highlighting any and all positive results. They should be embracing and trying programs like "Moonshot Mondays," always understanding that while their initial efforts may be tentative and imperfect, they are heading in the right direction for their kids and for the world.

TEACHER EDUCATORS

Individuals responsible for teacher preparation and for in-service training of teachers are in a particularly influential position. They ought to be looking for what they can add to their programs that will prepare teachers for the changes that are coming. Education schools should be already be developing and offering programs and preparation in Bettering Their World skills of empowering students, and coaching real-world project teams, getting those programs certified for credits and inclusion in licensure. This is a big but exciting task.

MEMBERS OF THE GENERAL PUBLIC INTERESTED IN, AND INVESTED IN, OUR FUTURE

Members of the public who are interested in our society's future—whether they have kids of their own still in school or not—need to think carefully about the kinds of education that will ensure our kids', our countries', and our world's success in our new age. All who agree with the thesis of this book—i.e., that the education we need for the future is not the academic education of the past but an accomplishment-based, Better Their World education of the future—need to begin advocating and lobbying for change. Everyone, including business, government, and nongovernmental organization leaders, and members, should begin thinking about the problems that students could solve at various levels, and sharing them with our schools.

As citizens, we must not permit those who equate "better education" with "more of the past done better" to remain unchallenged—whether those people be intellectuals, the press, groups of parents, or anyone else. If we do, our education and our kids will make little progress.

YOUNG PEOPLE

I have saved young people for last because they are the most important group of all, and I very much hope there are young people among my readers. Today, more and more kids feel trapped—impaled, in many cases—between what their parents' generation insists they need as an education, and what they feel strongly is right for them in these times in which they now find themselves.

Most kids want to be with, and work with, their peers and equals, and to fully become the people they have the potential to be—which is why they want to go to the best schools and obtain the best jobs that they possibly can. But our young people also see brand new opportunities emerging quickly in their world, and too often feel stifled by their parents and others from reaching for those opportunities.

The most important thing I advocate, for both parents and kids, is frequent, mutually respectful dialogue about these issues. If you are a young person today, there are many things you can learn from your elders' experience. Yet your priorities and your decisions, whenever possible, ought to be based on your own needs and the needs you perceive in the world. More and more young people are telling me, and others, that their true desire is to "better their world." If that is, in fact, *your* desire as a young person, you should be clear that you are now truly empowered to do so, and can act on that desire in ways that were impossible in the past. I encourage you in the strongest possible terms to do so.

Education as Rocket Science: A New Metaphor

DESPITE SOME OF THE "DOOM AND GLOOM" we hear about today's kids—and even with our often alarming dropout rates—I don't think the situation is as bad as many fear. What we need to do to regain our optimism is to look at our kids differently.

Today, we far too often treat our kids as if they were, metaphorically, trains on a track to the future, when actually (again metaphorically) today's kids are really rockets.

Which, by the way, makes educators (yet again metaphorically) rocket scientists—Who knew?

What makes today's kids rockets? At first blush, it's their speed—they operate faster than any generation that has come before. Although little may have changed in the rate kids grow up emotionally, there has been enormous change in what today's kids learn and know at early ages, and, therefore, in the rate our kids grow up intellectually. "Kids getting older younger" is a term long in use by MTV. Although parents and educators struggle with getting kids to learn in the old sense, what they offer the kids is often *way behind* what the kids need. "Age appropriate" has totally outrun us. Even students of Piaget suggest it is time for a new look. While many want kids to slow down, speed is clearly their reality.

But what makes today's kids rockets is not just the increased speed. Like rockets, our kids are headed to far away destinations, places that often those who launch them can't even see. They have been designed—by their 21st-century upbringing, including the Internet, social media, and the complex games many play—to explore, and find out for themselves what works. Like rockets, they often cannot be controlled at every moment but are initially aimed, as best we can, in the right direction, with mid-course corrections to be made as necessary. And because both kids and rockets are difficult to repair in flight, they must be made as self-sufficient as possible.

As with all rockets, our kids' fuel mix is volatile. Some go faster and farther than others. Some lose their guidance or their ability to follow direction. Some go off course or stop functioning unexpectedly. Some even blow up. But many more hit their mark, and it is the job of the rocket scientists to help them do so.

Perhaps most importantly, today's rockets—and kids—can potentially go much further and do things far beyond what any such voyager could do in the past. With the arrival of widely distributed and easy-to-use digital tools, our kids already accomplish on a daily basis things that still seem, for many of us, far-off science fiction. They communicate instantaneously with, and learn from, other kids around the globe— the Internet now reaches every country and territory. They regularly make videos and post them for the world to see and comment on. They organize themselves socially and politically across and throughout the planet. The pollster Zogby calls our rocket kids "The Globals," but "The Galactics" is perhaps an even better name. Most of today's kids realize this at some level, even though many of the adults in their lives don't.

EDUCATORS AS ROCKET SCIENTISTS

What does this imply for those whose job it is to educate today's kids— kids who can fly around the globe and beyond, further and faster than we ever thought possible? It tells us that we must conceive of what educators do in a new metaphorical way—not as teachers, but as rocket scientists, building and sending off the best rockets (i.e., students) we possibly can. This means, for one thing, not filling our rocket students up with the old educational fuel of the past, because that fuel just doesn't make today's kids go. We need new fuel, new designs, new boosters, and new payloads.

How do "real" rocket scientists prepare their charges for success? For one thing, they understand that their rockets will likely encounter many unforeseen events and trials, so they work hard to build into the rockets' "brains" (i.e., their software) enough intelligence to get the job done with the minimum of outside help. They build into the rockets the ability to self-monitor, to self-assess, and to self-correct as much as possible. They create the ability for their rockets to use whatever devices and instrumentation are available to regularly gather data and then analyze it, even as they are speeding along. They perform rigid quality control, not of what the rockets' brains know—that's updatable on the fly—but of what they can do with the information they encounter. And while they may preprogram a target, they know that the target will likely change mid-course, and that there are likely to be other changes during the course of the rocket's life.

A USEFUL PERSPECTIVE

Seeing our students in this new way—i.e., as rockets—and ourselves as rocket scientists, is incredibly useful and helpful for educators—and all of us—to do. One key reason is that it encourages us to set the bar for student achievement extremely high—much higher than we typically do currently. I have often heard educators say that they were "blown away" by what their students accomplished. We should not be blown away by our students; we should be expecting *even more* from them.

Rockets are high maintenance and often require more of our effort and skills to build and keep up. They are also useless on the ground, so that is not where we should be preparing them to stay (many of the "ground skills," having been taken over by machines, are no longer needed).

EXPLORATION OR DESTRUCTION?

Depending on the payload installed in their heads at the beginning of the journey, our kids (like real rockets) can be powerful forces for exploration and change or potential weapons of destruction. Educators (along with parents) install the payload in the rockets that are our kids. Then, they send them off to fly into the future, hoping they have prepared them well for what they will meet. To make the payloads positive, installing ethical behavior—the ability to figure out the right thing to do and to get it done—ought to be one of our top concerns as "rocket scientist" educators. We need to best configure students' brains so they can constantly learn, create, program, adopt, adapt, accomplish, and relate positively to whatever and whomever they meet (and in whatever way they meet them, which increasingly means through technology).

We want our kids, like rockets, to "boldly go where no one has gone before." Surprisingly, for this to happen the most important changes required of educators are not technological but rather conceptual—thinking of themselves not as guardians of the past, but as rocket scientists guiding their living, breathing "rockets," as partners, toward the future. No one—certainly not me—advocates throwing away the past completely. But unless we start preparing our kids to fly much farther than before and land safely, we won't be doing them much good. If we don't soon start putting some new and different fuel and payloads into the rockets that are in our charge, then (once more metaphorically) our students will never get off the ground.

It is time to give all our kids the education they deserve.

Frequently Voiced
(and Unvoiced) Concerns

As I present the ideas in this book around the world, many of the same objections and questions are brought up over and over again by audiences. They are often stated as what I call **"Yes . . . buts"** (as in "**Yes,** Marc, I totally agree with you in principal, **but** in *my* school [or state, or country] we have . . .) I'd like to address several of these "Yes . . . buts" here, in case they have formed in your mind as you read the book.

YES . . . BUT DON'T KIDS STILL NEED "THE BASICS"?

Yes, young people do still need to acquire basic, foundational skills. But the basic skills they need are changing radically and dramatically in our times, and the speed at which this change is happening is something we often don't realize or want to accept. The skills that have been basic to our success, and to the success of most graduates in our times, will be quite different by the time most of today's primary school kids grow up. If we expend our efforts today on providing our kids the same basic skills that were provided to us, they will be radically unequipped for their own times.

This goes far beyond just adding a few 21st century or social/emotional skills to our existing curricula. It means rethinking everything we do—and don't do. It means recognizing the rising importance of video and the fading primacy of text in all communications. It means recognizing that arithmetical calculation is no longer the kind of mathematics people need. It means recognizing that the "basics" and "basic curriculum" we offer kids today, in almost every school and subject, is really an extremely narrow set of knowledge and skills—overly detailed in every case—that is, with few exceptions, neither necessary nor in any sense "basic" to most lives for the future. It means recognizing that we *don't* offer our kids a great many of the basics, they really do need, i.e. an easily learned and remembered set of crucial knowledge and skills in all the important areas of thinking, acting, relating and accomplishing that we already, as collective humanity, know a lot about. We require a huge rethinking of the "basics" we offer in order to prepare our children adequately for their future.

YES . . . BUT DON'T KIDS HAVE TO "KNOW STUFF"? WHAT IF THEY WANT TO BE A DOCTOR?

When someone intends to specialize in a professional field, such as medicine, they certainly need a wide variety and deep set of knowledge and skills. This is, in fact, what "higher education" is for—it is, or ought to be, for kids who have acquired in their K–12 years, in addition to the basic skills of thinking, acting, relating, and accomplishing, a clear idea of what they want to do, and who are motivated and willing to work hard for that. What all kids need in their primary and secondary education, almost more than anything else (and certainly more than the knowledge, and even skills, we offer today), is our help in discovering where their personal interests, strengths, and passions lie, and in figuring out how and where they can best apply those passions and strengths to the rest of their life.

YES . . . BUT IF KIDS JUST FOLLOW THEIR PASSIONS, WON'T THEY BE MISSING OUT ON EXPOSURE TO OTHER THINGS?

We may think that we do a good job of exposing kids to potential interests and opportunities, but in reality we do not, because we do it in such a random and narrow fashion (often based, for example, on what teachers one happens to get). Although helping kids find what in the world they are passionate about is very important, what our kids also need to acquire from us is how to *apply* whatever passion they may have at a given time to accomplishing useful things that improve their world. Today our schools, with few exceptions, do an extremely poor job of helping kids find their passions and of helping kids apply them usefully in the world. Real-world projects—especially with kids taking on various roles as they do them—will do a far better job of exposing kids to a greater variety of possibilities. A huge part of every

K–12 educators' time ought to be spent on helping kids identify their own interests, strengths and passions, and connecting them with fields, people, and projects, where those passions can be further explored and new ones discovered.

YES . . . BUT CAN EVERYTHING KIDS NEED BE ACQUIRED THROUGH A REAL, WORLD-IMPROVING PROJECT-BASED APPROACH?

It can and should. Doing so, moreover, will make it far more likely that students—motivated by the needs of their projects and passions—will want to investigate and learn about particular areas and skills in depth. Two key differences between the education of today and the emerging vision of education described in this book are that (1) in the future vision the content of of a person's education—i.e. the projects chosen—is determined by the students' own needs (as determined with guidance from their educators) rather than by fiat from above, and (2) it is no longer necessary, for knowledge and skills to be applied effectively, for all students to go through a common progression of linear courses in advance of doing anything useful. An analogy for this change might be acquiring a second language in a course versus acquiring that language as you live in a new country. Courses help, for sure, but in an ancillary, rather than a primary way. In almost all cases, the primary and best way to build knowledge and skill is interacting with the real-world.

YES . . . BUT WERE WE TO DROP "THE MESS" WOULDN'T KIDS BE DEPRIVED OF MUCH OF IMPORTANCE?

If we just ensure our kids get a "basic minimum" of the MESS subjects (really very little and mostly top level)—and get much more of what is currently missing from our MESS based curricula—I believe they will be deprived of nothing of true importance. We need, in this age of abundant information, to focus on "compression" and on getting kids to the essence of what we want them to know. To me it is far preferable, for example, that all U.S. kids know that the history of the United States is, at its core, "Native people, European immigrants, a political experiment, continental expansion, slavery, civil war, economic success, world leadership, ongoing issues" (that's just 153 characters, including commas and spaces—slightly more than a tweet), than that they know who Christopher Columbus was, or in what exact year he came. Today most kids who have studied history couldn't give you that big picture, because most of what we offer kids today is detail. What if all our kids could give you such an arc for each of the major countries and regions of the world—would that not be more useful and important? Our MESS-based curricula offer far too many facts and far too little context or application—I urge you to think about just how much of the subject matter you learned in K–12 you have ever used used in your daily or work life. Today kids can take "socialstudies" for 13 years without realizing, or ever being told, that it is "the study of peoples" (that was the case for me). Kids can spend huge amounts of time doing calculations that a chip costing less than one cent can now do, without understanding how to evaluate the appropriateness of their answer (which the chip doesn't know). Kids can be forced to read literature they find boring or outdated without ever knowing that the reason we do so is to learn about enduring human relationships. We would do much more for our kids by offering them far "less of the MESS"—and far more of its "essence."

YES . . . BUT WHAT WOULD THE "BETTER THEIR WORLD" "CURRICULUM" ACTUALLY CONSIST OF, AND HOW WOULD WE TEACH IT?"

What a "Better Their World" education will expect all K–12 kids to accomplish in order to become educated is a continuous series of world-improving team tasks and projects—a different mix for each student—all of which improve their world in some meaningful way. Those projects will be supported by a large set of underlying skills—not just thinking skills, but also action, relationship and accomplishment skills—that we'd like all our kids to acquire over their K–12 years. This education will teach kids not just that these key skills exist, but also their essential elements—in ways that *because they have used them in practical applications*, they will retain for the test of their lives. Our kids will no longer be taught a narrow range of subjects in a pre-determined linear order in "courses," nor will the skills they need be acquired by all students at once (i.e., "just in case"). They will be acquired, rather, individually, by each student, as needed (i.e., "just in time").

YES . . . BUT ISN'T WHAT YOU ADVOCATE JUST A WESTERN, UPPER-CLASS VISION FOR KIDS WITH THE LATEST TECHNOLOGY?

Not at all—it is a vision for the entire world. Although most of the projects I have citied as examples in this book are from the U.S., similar kinds of projects are taking place everywhere—I am collecting them in the database at globalempoweredkids.org. What kids do and can do today is very similar in places from New York, to Paris, to Shanghai, to Kuala Lumpur. Rural areas are fast catching up. Moreover, as I pointed out in Chapter 10, although technology does empower kids, an Education to Better Their World does not *require* technology at all. Many projects, such as clean-ups, or improving people's lives, can be done entirely without technology. Where technology is truly needed, or helpful it can often be provided by NGOs, companies and even governments. Education to Better Their World is a vision for *all* kids.

YES . . . BUT IS THERE ENOUGH IN A "BETTER THEIR WORLD" EDUCATION TO KEEP KIDS USEFULLY ENGAGED FOR UP TO 13 YEARS?

There is more than enough. First, most of the work consists of world-improving projects, which we will never run out of. Second all the skills of effective thinking, action, relationships and accomplishment (see the lists in Chapter 9) are lifelong, and will be continuously acquired in more depth, in the same way as a serious musician constantly and continuously improves their many skills.

YES . . . BUT WHAT ABOUT ASSESSMENT AND EVALUATION?

Assessment can be useful when done right, but most of our so-called "assessments" are really attempts at "ranking," which is not necessary and often harmful. In school, and in business, we really need only three categories of assessment and evaluation, i.e., *competent* (which is, typically most people—generally, in a group, around 75 percent), outstanding (generally around 10-15 percent), and *not yet competent* (generally around 10-15 percent)—people use a variety of names for these. Ranking is something that is impossible to do accurately or fairly (which is why we expend so much effort attempting to do it.). For admission into limited programs, those programs must formulate their own criteria, which most already do. It is actually far easier to assess and evaluate "accomplishment," where something either gets done or it doesn't, than it is to assess "academic achievement."

YES . . . BUT HOW DO WE DEAL WITH THE HUGE NUMBER OF CURRENT TENURED TEACHERS UNTRAINED IN THIS NEW VISION OF EDUCATION? CAN WE RETRAIN THE WORLD'S ENTIRE CORPS OF TEACHERS?

Change is coming to all professions—including teaching. We should deal with teachers just as we do with all professionals in our changing world—be they doctors, lawyers, or architects—by respecting their experience yet also putting them on the new paths they have to take, through training and example. One big difference between the teaching profession and many other professions is that teachers' clients are not their own contemporaries, but rather our kids. This alone should be, for those who care deeply about young people, sufficient reason to start changing to a more forward-looking vision of education. We must work with teachers both by putting them in new situations (with support), and by offering them different preparation. And we also must also be ready, just as we do with other professions, to *require* all our teachers to take the new paths, sooner rather than later, by changing not only our teacher preparation, but also our licensure and certification requirements to reflect our evolving situation.

YES . . . BUT WILL A REAL-WORLD ACCOMPLISHMENT-BASED EDUCATION ENABLE (OR HELP) MY KID TO GET IN TO A GOOD COLLEGE OR UNIVERSITY?

Colleges and universities—and even the definition of a "good" college or university—are now changing enormously and rapidly as those institutions face a growing tsunami of academic and economic pressures—higher ed is, in fact, changing far faster than K–12. Although some institutions are changing more quickly than others, already—at least in the U.S.—almost all top colleges and universities have taken, or are contemplating taking steps to admit students on far broader criteria than just grades and test scores—their admissions officers look increasingly for depth of real-world accomplishments on the part of applicants (state schools are slower in this regard). Already, without some significant real-world accomplishment, just having top grades is no longer enough to get a student into the "best" colleges and universities. This will only increase.

YES . . . BUT WILL A REAL-WORLD ACCOMPLISHMENT-BASED EDUCATION ENABLE (OR HELP) MY KID TO GET A GOOD JOB AND HAVE A SUCCESSFUL CAREER?

The same applies, even more so, to jobs and employment. Google's website, for example, states that "We look for "team-oriented people *who can get things done*." (Italics mine.) Getting things done is just another term for "accomplishment." Today we hear executives in all industries say they are looking for employees who can think critically, be innovative, and solve problems. Underlying this is the knowledge that if their employees can't accomplish and get things done, little else matters.

YES . . . BUT "IF THEY DON'T LEARN HISTORY, WON'T THEY JUST REPEAT IT?"

This final objection, that I hear frequently, is the most troubling of all to me. It is the same objection, in different words, as: "If our kids can't make change in their heads, won't all commerce come to a halt when the power goes down?" I hear this particular "Yes . . . but" continually from people who are convinced that one particular subject or method from the past or today (e.g. history, math, writing, "Socratic discussion" or "deep textual analysis) is what all kids "really" need. My issue with this is not that these people are wrong to say that the subject or method they promote is important to some—or even many—students. Where they are wrong is in suggesting that a greatly disproportional amount of time should be spent, by all students, on whatever it is they support. My argument is, to a large extent, proportional—and needs to be— because we have, in the end, only a limited amount of time to prepare our kids for their future. We should certainly be spending some of that time on developing their thinking (as we do now) but we should be devoting at least equal time on developing action and relationship skills. And we should be devoting an even greater proportion of our kids' time to real, world-improving accomplishment, because it is so critical to their (and our) future. Obviously, this means modifying much of what we currently do. It means giving kids far more opportunity to pursue their own interests—whatever they may be—in depth, and in an applied, practical way, rather than on any curriculum decided from above.

We all want our kids to be educated. What is now changing, I believe, is what an "education" is, and what "being educated" means.

Notes

1. Zoe Weil is the founder of the Institute for Humane Education. She is also the author of the books *The World Becomes What We Teach (2016) and Most Good, Least Harm: A Simple Principle for a Better World and Meaningful Life* (2009). Her videos can be found online at www.humaneeducation.org/watch-zoe-weils-talk/

2. Marley Dias, age 11. On Jenna Bush Hagar's NBC Today show feature "Can-Do Kids," May 31 2016. http://www.today.com/parents/meet-girl-collecting-1000blackgirlbooks-libraries-schools-t95506

3. Singapore:
https://news.google.com/newspapers?nid=1309&dat=20010829&id=kiwhA AAAIBAJ&sjid=rXgFAAAAIBAJ&pg=4358,5317170&hl=en,

South Korea:
https://news.google.com/newspapers?nid=2209&dat=19880703&id=6xImAA AAIBAJ&sjid=xfwFAAAAIBAJ&pg=7291,781635&hl=en

Palo Alto, CA: https://www.washingtonpost.com/news/morning-mix/wp/2016/02/16/cdc-investigates-why-so-many-high-school-students-in-wealthy-palo-alto-have-committed-suicide/

4. Numerous articles on Five-0 have appeared in the press, including the *HuffPost Teen* of August 28, 2014 (www.huffingtonpost.com/2014/08/18/teens-police-brutality-app_n_5687934.html and the *Economist* of December 28, 2015 (www.economist.com/news/united-states/21684687-high-school-students-want-citizens-rate-their-interactions-officers-how-three).

5. Three-dimensional (3D) prosthetic hands, the printing of which has been promoted by the site www.enablethefuture.org, have also been printed by students for students in Widbey, WA (www.whidbeynewstimes.com/news/328738521.html#) and in other schools. The idea has also spread to colleges: Seattle's first annual Handathon was hosted by the University of Washington's Ability and Innovation lab in 2015.

6. Yoni Kalin, then 16, took an entrepreneurship course at Learn Serve International, which he credits as helping him develop his idea of redistributing used crayons into a large scale operation.

7. The fourth-grade class was in North Platte, MO. The superintendent at the time was David Engle. The class divided into teams, and then came to a consensus on the design it wanted. They then lobbied the local city council who accepted their ideas and got them integrated into the professional architectural plans.

8. The instructor who first described the need to the students in the internship classes he led, was Heriberto Reynoso. See www.themonitor.com/mvtc/news/wisd-students-building-robot-capable-of-cleaning-world-s-largest/article_e0614650-bbbb-11e5-b7b6-9f33bde11ac3.html

9. The district was Port Townsend, WA, under the leadership of superintendent David Engle. Through the Maritime Discovery Schools Initiative that he started, Engle helped forge close ties between the maritime-oriented local community (home of the annual Wooden Boat Festival), the Northwest Maritime Center, the Marine Science Center, the "Sound Experience" project and its wooden boat "Adventurer," and the Port Townsend public schools.

10. I heard about this personally from a school administrator. It is, however, the one project I haven't been able to track down specifically. If you know about this, please contact me. As soon as I do track it down, I will post the reference online.

11. The kids were in engineering classes at Castle View High School in Douglas County, CO, taught by Robert Hazelhurst. A video of the kids presenting the project is at www.dcsdk12.org/community-relations/job-alike-robotic-students

12. The 6-year-old was Ryan Hreljac. Information on Ryan and the foundation he started can be found at www.ryanswell.ca.

13. This project took place at High Tech High in San Diego. It was described to the author on a personal visit to the school.

14. www.youtube.com/watch?v=oQWGCnq6Cgo.

15. Kids in Haiti learned to repair broken traffic lights.

16. The 11-year-old cryptographer (whose name is kept secret for obvious reasons) was described to me by a friend with top-level security clearance.

17. Ashoka (ashoka.org) is a non-governmental, not-for-profit organization whose mission is "to advance an Everyone a Changemaker world where anyone can apply the skills of changemaking to complex social problems."

18. Contained in a personal email from Vint Cerf.

19. Once the databases and methodologies are in place, the next step will be to create a mechanism to help students identify their passions and strengths, and a dedicated "recommendation engine"—something we are already good at creating—to connect students to projects and roles of appropriate scope and level, to help them advance. Such projects are already under development.

20. https://www.teenlife.com/blogs/50-community-service-ideas-teen-volunteers. Accessed January, 2016. Used with permission.

21. A Google search for "passion-based education" on June 3, 2016 returned 79,500,000 results. "Passion-based learning" returned 70,700,000 results.

22. LRNG is a start-up, grown out of and funded in part by the Macarthur Foundation, to unite and expand the after-school opportunities in cities and communities. In many of the cases there are real-world projects involved. See www.lrng.org

23. 12-year-old 7th grader Abby Goldberg, in Chicago, was upset to discover discovered that Illinois lawmakers had passed a proposal requiring plastic-bag recycling programs and prohibiting municipalities from banning

or charging for them—a bill supported by the industry and opposed by environmentalists. She lobbied Governor Pat Quinn, collected allies and signatures, and was instrumental in getting the bill vetoed. The Chicago Tribune wrote: "After her yearlong crusade and an online campaign dubbed "Don't Let Big Plastic Bully Me," the northwest suburban girl is celebrating Quinn's decision to veto legislation that would have prevented cities and towns in Illinois from banning plastic bags and imposing fees on their use." http://articles.chicagotribune.com/2012-08-27/news/ct-met-plastic-bag-bill-veto-20120827_1_plastic-bag-abby-goldberg-pat-quinn.

24. The Saber-Tooth Curriculum parody, written under what I believe to be a pseudonym (J. Abner Pediwell), was first published in 1939. It is worth reading the relatively short original, but for those who can't, the gist is that ancient cave men developed a curriculum to teach kids "the basics" of catching fish in the clear pools, clubbing woolly horses for their food and warm skins, and using fire to protect themselves from saber-toothed tigers. When the environment changed radically—the pools became muddy, the horses migrated to other places, and the tigers died out and were replaced by bears unafraid of fire—the elders kept on teaching the old curriculum because it had become "traditional" and sacred, even though it was no longer of any use whatsoever.

25. Tanz, Jason. "The End of Code: Soon We Won't Program Our Computers. We'll Train Them" *Wired*, 24:06, June 2016.

26. de Bono, E. (1985) *Six Thinking Hats: An Essential Approach to Business Management*, Boston, Little, Brown & Co.

27. Covey, S. R. (1989) *The 7 Habits of Highly Effective People: Powerful Lessons in Personal Change*, New York, Simon & Schuster.

28. Duckworth, A. (2016) *Grit : The Power of Passion and Perseverance*, New York, Scribner.

29. http://www.nytimes.com/2013/09/15/magazine/can-emotional-intelligence-be-taught.html?pagewanted=all&_r=0

30. https://www.edsurge.com/news/2015-12-21-christmas-bonus-us-edtech-sets-record-with-1-85-billion-raised-in-2015

31. https://www.techinasia.com/talk/edtech-startups-fail

32. The Innovator's Dilemma, a concept originated by Professor Clayton Christensen of the Harvard Business School, states that companies often continue innovating to improve their current products on the margin, but get blindsided by new "disruptive" startups that deliver equivalent, better, or sufficient functionality at much lower cost.

33. Wojcicki, E. and Izumi, L. (2014). *Moonshots in Education: Blended leaning in the classroom*. San Francisco, CA: Pacific Research Institute.

34. Reported in R. Beckhard and R T. Harris (1977). *Organizational transitions: Managing complex change* (1st ed.)

35. As reported in S. H. Cady, J. Jacobs, R. Koller, and J. Spalding (2014). The change formula: Myth, legend, or lore. *OD Practitioner, 46(3)*, 32–39.

36. See https://www.youtube.com/watch?v=8xe6nLVXEC0#t=174.

About the Author

Marc Prensky, coiner of the term "Digital Native" in 2001, is currently the founder and Executive Director of the Global Future Education Foundation and Institute—a not-for-profit organization dedicated to promoting "Global Empowered Kids" and "Empowering Kids to Better Their World."

Marc has spoken in 40 countries. He has authored seven books, published over 100 essays, and his writings have been translated into 11 languages. Marc's background includes master's degrees from Harvard and Yale, six years at the Boston Consulting Group, software game development, and teaching at all levels. Marc's writings and speaking schedule can be found at www.marcprensky.com.

Contact Marc at marcprensky@gmail.com. See global-future-education.org, globalempoweredkids.org and bettertheirworld.org for more information.